RITES OF PASSAGE

FEATHERWORKS
PUBLICATIONS

TAMPA

RITES OF PASSAGE

Christlit
Book Award
2025

RAISING SONS TO BE
MEN OF STANDARD

SONYA D. FERREIRA

Rites of Passage: Raising Sons to be Men of Standard

Copyright © 2025 by Sonya D. Ferreira

Published by Featherworks Publications

Cover and book designed by David Ferreira

Printed in the United States of America.

For more information:
Featherworks Publications
Tampa, FL

Ferreira, Sonya D.
Rites of passage / Sonya D. Ferreira

ISBN 979-8-9905804-1-1 (Hardcover)
ISBN 979-8-9905804-0-4 (Paperback)
ISBN 979-8-9905804-2-8 (eBook)

Library of Congress Control Number: 2025934193

Second Edition

Shout for Joy

to the Lord, all the earth.

Worship the LORD with gladness.
Come before Him with

Joyful Songs.

KNOW THAT THE LORD IS

GOD

IT IS HE WHO MADE US, AND WE ARE HIS
WE ARE HIS PEOPLE,

THE SHEEP OF HIS PASTURE

Enter His gates with

THANKSGIVING

and His courts with praise.

GIVE THANKS TO HIM

and praise His name.

For the Lord is good and His love endures forever,

HIS FAITHFULNESS CONTINUES THROUGH ALL GENERATIONS.

Psalm 100

MY INSPIRATION

"I will climb up to my watchtower and stand at my guardpost. There I will wait to see what the Lord says and how He will answer my complaint. Then the Lord said to me, write My answer plainly on tablets, so that a runner can carry the correct message to others."

Habakkuk 2:1-2

I am inspired by the gospel of Jesus Christ. The principles in Holy Scripture are so rich with solutions to living and overcoming trying times. The intent of this writing is to elevate the importance of instilling respect for spiritual authority in parenting and honoring a boy's passage into manhood and leadership. I am humbled to put ink to paper in this message of hope and unity while sharing my life experiences with others. Thank you, Abba!

I also write to acknowledge the rites of passage for my sons, Elijah and Ephraim Ferreira, and their patience with me being a student of my sons. I pray for them to reach their highest potential and realize the magnificent men of valor residing inside of them. May they love their wives, their children, and humanity enough to lead and fight for them.

Finally, I dedicate this book to the universal and sacrificial devotion of mothers around the world. Meme, Ema, Mama, Nanay, Anm, Madre – however, mother is pronounced in any language, it means something special to the hearer. It is a labor of love to raise our sons into men of standard. A mother may work long hours in the marketplace and then transform into the Chief Executive Officer of the home, managing household responsibilities, school commitments, and extracurricular activities. Mothers are primary teachers, coaches, chauffeurs, playmates, comforters, prayer warriors, and so much more on behalf of their children. I marvel as I observe mothers performing all the routine tasks that are needed just in the course of a single week. There is no one like a mother.

For the spiritual mothers, women who nurture and guide children they did not birth but love just the same, this book is for you too. I celebrate the Aunties, Big Mommas, Nanas, Abuelas, and Big Sisters who stand in the gap or assist struggling women in loving, providing for, and protecting their children. Love, as we know it, could not exist without a sacrificial heart, so I honor all kinds of 'mothers' throughout the generations.

My sisters, I encourage you to stand your ground and NEVER give up hope for our children! They need us to become the change our world needs. Thank you for your sacrifices.

In Gratia
(With Gratitude)

"And my tongue shall speak of Your righteousness and of Your praise all the day long." (NKJV)

Psalm 35:28

I have many reasons to express gratitude, and indeed, I am grateful to those who were an integral part of my life story and to those yet to play a role in my destiny. While I cannot name everyone, there are some people to whom I must pay tribute.

My husband, Dave – It is reassuring to walk in a threefold covenant. Thank you for being a loving father, always there for our sons, especially when I was away. Loyalty is one of your greatest attributes and you remained steadfast through the different seasons of marriage. Thank you for all your efforts in producing this work. I love you, always!

My sons, Elijah and Ephraim – Mommy did not always get it 'right,' but I did the best I could at the time. Thank you for your understanding as I developed more into the mother I was meant to be. You are worth every sacrifice I have made and will ever make. My devotion to your well-being will remain a priority until my last breath. I will always fight for you!

My Spiritual Sons, Quintin Payton, Elijah "EJ" Bell, and Jamahdia "Madi" Whitby – I encountered you as children and now you are young men. Through the sleepovers, hangouts, and family trips, you are forever part of my family. I share in your mother's joy knowing the outstanding men you have become.

My mom, Pamela M. Jordan – Without you, there could be no me. As the years go by, I am learning the value of mothering and appreciate you all the more. I love you!

My grandmother, Mary E. Hansley – I appreciate all the sacrifices you made during my early childhood years. The time you spent investing in me was foundational to becoming the person I am today. Thank you!

George "Pop" Walton and Lucille "Mom" Walton (in memoriam) – You gave me an understanding of what it means to have a spiritual family by showing me the way I should go. You took my family in as your own from day one. Your loving kindness (and correction) in the infancy years of marriage created a bedrock that we continue to stand on today. Love you to eternity!

My goddaughter, Bria Williams – I watched you grow into an honorable and amazing young lady with a heart for worshiping the Lord. I pray this book inspires you to seek an honorable man to treat you as the one-of-a-kind, precious gem you are. I am so proud of you!

My Spiritual Parents – Archbishop David M. Copeland and Rev. Dr. Claudette Copeland – Your consistency in modeling Christ-like character and raising spiritual children to know Jesus was a game-changer. Under your spiritual care, I was equipped to run my race and maintain my integrity, even when it cost me. I was abandoned by some, but never by God. My discipleship time with you is one of my most prized possessions. Thank you for your faithfulness in season and out of season. I love you for who you are and all you epitomize in the Kingdom of God!

My Extended Family – God poured out mercy into the relationships He orchestrated, from Maryland to Texas to Arizona to Virginia and every place in between. Thank you for your belief in me and all the 'jack-up' conversations when I needed them. Your wisdom kept me from derailing my family and I am indebted to you for your unconditional love. I pray you know your investment in me was not in vain.

My Kingdom Family – There are more than I can name but First Missionary Baptist Church (Lexington Park, MD), New Creation Christian Fellowship (San Antonio, TX), Harvest Land Ministries (Hampton, VA), Grace Family Church (Tampa, FL), and Deeper Fellowship Church (Orlando, FL) remain places of hope, strength, and kindness towards my family. The Kingdom of God has many houses of worship and I continue to live out of the overflow from being connected to such ministries. Thank you for being a part of my spiritual community and supporting me through hills and valleys.

To all my Family and Friends – You provided guidance, aid, and inspiration to birth this book, so thank you is not enough. Your prayers and words of encouragement during some challenging times meant more than you will ever know. Thank you for holding my hand while I was laboring to make it to the finish line.

To my Support Team – I appreciate the feedback from readers and editors who reviewed and helped me revise this work so it could come to fruition. Special thanks to Robin Page, Karen Gregory, Diane Weller, and Miguel and Melanie Martinez. Your perspective helped me refine my thoughts into better writing.

Participants in the Ferreira Rites of Passage – Reverend James and Bridgette Harris, Pastor Michael and LaKer Barber, Alfred and Carmen Meyers, Pastor Dwane and Indera Cardenas, Philip and Robin Page, Pastor Lee and Camicia Evans, and Dexter and Tiffany Godfrey – your presence blessed and humbled me. I am grateful for your acts of generosity and love. Muchas Gracias, Te Amo!

> *O Lord my God, you have performed many wonders for us. Your plans for us are too numerous to list. You have no equal. If I tried to recite all your wonderful deeds, I would never come to the end of them.*

Psalm 40:5

CONTENTS

What Others Are Saying About
Rite of Passage
Ceremonies

Manhood Elevation

Several years ago, two of my best friends invited me to witness what they called a Rite of Passage for their son, Elijah. It was by far the best thing I witnessed that year. They brought together a collection of men who were instrumental in their son's upbringing to bestow on him the elevation to manhood. As men, we are thrust into the role of manhood, never being told when that certain time arrives. The Rite of Passage was a ceremony of elevation, letting Elijah know IT'S TIME! It is something every young man should experience, as it eliminates the question of when they transition. I was honored to share in the opportunity to witness this event, and if given the chance, I will definitely have a Rite of Passage ceremony with my grandsons. Hats off to Team Ferreira as they always pave the way in truly showing how to live on purpose!

Alfred Meyers –
Author, Grief - The Silent Assassin

The Rite of Passage was not an event, it was an experience. An experience that allowed my family to reflect on

1

what was, is, and will be in the life of our offspring. It is an emblem for all young men to encounter because it expresses the transition from adolescence to adulthood in high definition. It is a twenty-first-century passing of the mantle.

Pastor Michael P. Barber –
Founder, One Dominion Movement

The Rite of Passage event was life-changing for me. As a mother of two sons, it was refreshing to see both Sonya and David speak words of life over Elijah in addition to men of God who laid hands on him. This impartation from family, friends, and the community demonstrated the love and support of a village. My goal is to do something similar for our sons because I know everyone who took part in this ceremony, including myself, felt the presence of God for greater purpose and destiny, and we will never be the same.

Tiffany Godfrey –
Speaker, Trainer, and Wife Coach

I have known Sonya for over 30 years. She is a thoughtful writer and serious thinker who translated her wisdom into practical insights to demonstrate the power of elevating and honoring young men through Rite of Passage ceremonies. I encourage you to listen and receive new revelation through her words as I have done many times in my life.

Reverend James F. Harris –
Senior Pastor, New Life Missionary Baptist Church

AUTHOR'S DECLARATIONS

I believe in and accept the Bible as Holy Scriptures, the Truth, and my standard for living.

I believe there are spiritual principles and forces at work in our world, some support our families and others are against them, so parents must protect their children and equip them to be strong and courageous.

I believe God demonstrates grace and mercy to all people, even those who do not acknowledge Him; His grace compels me to be more compassionate and kind.

I believe listening to understand people with different perspectives, backgrounds, and experiences cause us to examine ourselves for alignment of our words, actions, and beliefs.

I believe change is inevitable, but growth is an intentional act made by choice.

I do not believe in a zero-sum mentality in parenting – focusing on the value of mother-son relationships is not intended to compare, negate, or degrade the value of father-son relationships. Both are necessary and complementary.

"The best and most beautiful things in the world cannot be seen or even touched – they must be felt with the heart."

Helen Keller

RITES OF PASSAGE

A LETTER TO MOTHERS OF SONS

*"It is easier to build strong children
than to repair broken men."*

Frederick Douglas

My Dear Sisters,

It is both a rewarding and daunting prospect to raise godly and honorable men in our global culture. I suspect every generation has its challenges with bringing up moral and respectable men in their society, so this assignment is not unique to us in this day. We should find comfort in knowing we are a part of a great cloud of mothers who have gone before us. They produced men of standard and integrity who became husbands, fathers, brothers, and leaders who changed our world. We can and must be agents of change for future generations.

When I finally submitted to the idea of being a mother (more on that later), I desired to have at least one daughter, but that was not to be. I am a mother of sons, amazing young men who have a world to take on. Very few mothers have the angelic encouragement like Mary, mother of Jesus, who received a direct message about the purpose of her soon-to-be son. Most women become mothers knowing we do not fully know what to expect. We may have gaps in our knowledge and lack understanding of the complexities and transitions involved in such a great responsibility.

I share this with you, my Sisters fighting in the battle for the hearts and minds of our sons. We are powerful beyond measure, but we have to believe we are empowered to fulfill our mandate – to produce young men who become righteous leaders. It is our job to help our sons identify and embrace their purpose. There is no better gift that sons can give to their mothers than to let them know they have raised sons who are men of standard.

This book may bring insight to fathers, some of whom are struggling and were never properly fathered themselves. God wants men to lean into their divine authority and lift the standard of manhood. My library consists of books written for men by men like John Eldridge, Dr. Tony Evans, and Steve Farrar. I read books focused on teaching men to be leaders in their families first, then in their communities. Why? Because I have sons who I expect to develop into great men in their families and communities. It really takes a village, with different experiences and perspectives; I cannot do it alone. We were not meant to go through this journey alone.

I was not created to think like a father raising a son. I am a mother, a mother of sons. I have the capacity to mother in partnership with their father and those who have a vested interest in them. I pray this writing will fan the flames of the mother's heart and challenge us to take authority as we continue walking in our calling!

With Compassion,

Tonya

PREFACE

Some people may think, "I am not a mother or I don't believe in God so this book does not apply to me." I would ask you to reconsider for two reasons. First, you are probably a part of some community with some influence. You may be a teacher, coach, pastor, supervisor, parent, civic leader, or another authority figure. Therefore, you have influence on someone and a responsibility to future generations. The core message of this book speaks to character, legacy, and those who are willing to say: "I will help raise our young men to be leaders of leaders in a world that is desperate for good leadership."

Second, I have encountered many people who are not believers in Jesus or hold different spiritual convictions, but they have been companions. Growth is produced through various experiences if we are open to listening to learn about others. We can discover how to communicate and live across differences with civility and respect. In the process, our perspectives may broaden and change. More importantly, this sharing creates opportunities for further exploration of our hearts and walking in kindness towards those who are different than us.

In his devotional, Dr. Tony Evans describes this mindset with great mastery: "Jehovah El Elohim the Lord God of Gods does not force what society calls Christianity on anyone. He invites people to partake in an encounter with Him that leads to a new life experience with Him. People have tried to force the Bible, God, and religious dogma on others…it will always be met with resistance when people feel forced to do anything. Instead, I offer the invitation to try and see for yourself. If you accept the Lord, Adonai, as God then it should be of your own volition. There is no other way to come to Him but in a posture of humility in the spirit of truth. This same posture is required when sharing the goodness of God with others. It is not for judging or condemnation but for inviting all to have their own experience with the Lord, if they choose. If they do not, *love them anyway* because that is what Jesus does!"[i]

This perspective, of loving people and respecting our differences enough to care for others who are different, is exactly what our world needs. It is easy to dream and talk about making the world a better place, but what steps are we willing to take to actually do it?

"You must be the change you wish to see in the world."

Mohanda Karamchand (Mahatma) Ghandi

CHAPTER 1
ENTER THE
RITES OF PASSAGE
WHO WOULD HAVE THUNK?

"For I know the plans I have for you," says the Lord. "They are plans for good and not for disaster, to give you a future and a hope."

Jeremiah 29:11

The lion rules over the pride, but the lioness trains the cubs so they can survive and develop into the leaders they are destined to be. She is a fierce warrior and defender of her cubs. She protects, nurtures, and produces the next generation of leaders in the pride.

In 1997, I was serving in the United States Air Force as an active duty officer. It was my first duty assignment with my new husband of one week, Dave. We had some bumps, but we made San Antonio, Texas into what we now consider our second home. It is a wonderful city with loving people who embraced a young military couple just starting their marriage journey. We had no clue what to expect or even how to be married, much less how to live together in a city without any family or friends, but that was about to change.

9

Fast-forward a couple years, and we'd developed an awesome support system of extended family and friends through church, work, and community. Life was good; not perfect, but good. We were thankful. I'd just completed my master's degree from St. Mary's University and was focusing on building a professional career in marriage and family counseling, after military life, but...

With all of our scientific advancements, it is critical to realize people still have limitations, and comprehending the works of the divine is one of those limits.

On a Saturday night in September 2001, I had a strange dream. It was strange for two reasons. First, although people dream every night, most do not recall their dreams and I was in that category. Second, I not only recalled my dream, it was so vivid that it seemed like I was truly experiencing it. When I awoke, I wasn't sure if it was only a dream, but for the sake of argument, let's say it *was* only a dream.

The next morning, my husband and I headed to church. On the ride, I shared my strange dream with Dave. I told him how I saw us standing in the church service on the front row. It was a high time of worship, and our hands were lifted and our eyes closed. As I worshiped, the Bishop walked through the service and I felt him place his left hand on my right side, very quickly, as he passed by, declaring to me, "You will have a son and his name will be Elijah." The dream ended with my retort: "Dave got to the Bishop!"

Before this message sounds too spiritual for some of you, I have to tell you, I was not seeing the spiritual side of this dream initially. I certainly was not considering or looking forward to motherhood. Somewhere in my heart and mind, I could not see me being a mother. I enjoyed the practice of mothering children as an auntie, godmother, and mentor, but actually giving birth to my own children…that was out of the question for me.

During that season, I was focused on my education and advancing my career. If the Government did not issue children to me, then I didn't need them…so the saying goes. At least, I did not need them yet. I saw the stress that military life puts on active-duty mothers. Women could leave their husbands for months but leaving their children, that was a different story. In my unlearned way of thinking, being a mother would only hinder my advancement and create competition for my time and energy. No thank you! I could experience similar joys from the periphery, so I deluded myself.

From a medical perspective, I thought I would not be able to bear children without significant complications in labor. My belief was based on a medical report I'd received in my teens, and my frame of reference for being a mother was inaccurately characterized by the polarized opinion of one well-intended medical professional. I must emphasize to medical professionals that the influence of the words spoken to young patients is immense. There is a responsibility to deliver them with extreme care. I would never suggest hiding the truth or

11

denying medical facts. However, facts are one type of information that does not always reveal the whole story.

With all of our scientific advancements, it is critical to realize people still have limitations, and comprehending the works of the divine is one of those limits. Words spoken to a tender heart can result in unintended consequences to those precious patients and the impact can be far-reaching, beyond what medical facts could possibly predict or conclude. So, a dose of humility and empathy should accompany the delivery of any medical prognosis. I wonder if I would have been such a staunch opponent to motherhood had I been given more empathetic medical counsel.

Now, imagine my shock when I heard the news! There I was, pregnant, and there was no going back. In the months preceding the birth of our first child, Dave began reading a novel called *The Book of God*. At that time, this particular book captivated him in a way I had not seen before. Frequently, he recounted passages of the book to me. In the beginning, it was interesting, but eventually I was sighing and rolling my eyes. "Not another passage, please!" Feeling like the Grinch at Christmas, what I disliked most of all was Dave retelling the story of Elijah, the prophet of God, over and over again.

So, back to that dream...Consider how I felt when the Bishop told me about a son that I did not plan and said the name I did not want to hear, Elijah. That crazy dream was a C-O-Nspiracy as far as I was concerned, and I was partially right! Within a week of having this dream, I began feeling different, much more sluggish and tired. It was abnormal for me since I was an early riser, actively exercised, and kept a pretty clean lifestyle. Finally, I thought I should visit the clinic to see if I was anemic or something. It was definitely *something!*

By that time, I was reassigned to Brooks Air Force Base, also in San Antonio but on the other side of the city. The medical clinic was small, and they were able to see me on short notice. They recommended running some tests to 'rule out' any major concerns. I agreed and upon the nurses' follow-up, I learned I was approximately two weeks pregnant.

Okay, I was not prepared for that news! First, who finds out they are pregnant at two weeks? Most women need at least one cycle to get an inkling, so two weeks is insanely early in the developmental process to have a doctor confirm pregnancy. Not to mention, the early detection caused me to feel like I was pregnant *forever*.

Second, the pregnancy was only confirming what God was communicating to me (preparing my heart) in the dream. Now faced with the medical facts and reliving the warning from my previous medical history, I felt hoodwinked and bamboozled, into motherhood of all things! Realizing a lot of my emotions were caused by my reactions to my thinking, I decided to get a grip. If I changed my thinking, I could change my perception and be more accepting of the coming reality.

Both Dave and I agreed we should not find out the baby's sex in advance (as if we did not already know we were having a son). Despite my dream, I secretly held out hope for a little girl. I envisioned shopping for dresses and styling hair with barrettes. These were little-girl experiences I'd never had with my mother. My upbringing had been unique, so maybe something in me yearned to experience those moments from a maternal viewpoint.

On June 8, 2002, at 11:42 pm in San Antonio, Texas at Lackland Air Force Base, my first son was born. We named him Elijah, just as my dream foretold. In the 41 weeks and 6 days of gestation, I'd had sufficient time to adjust my attitude about becoming a mom. If there was any consolation to be found, it was in knowing God is sovereign and He had a plan, but it was different from mine. Darn!

CHAPTER 2

PASSAGE OF UNCERTAINTY

NOW WHAT?

"What good would it be to get everything you want and lose you, the real you?"

Mark 8:36 (MSG)

Priorities! Ugh...So often, people have a hard time keeping the main thing – the MAIN thing. Contemporary gospel artist Toby Mac sings a song with the lyrics, "I don't want to gain the whole world and lose my soul." That's a profound thought I suspect most people choose not to think about, because we exist in an overly busy and overstimulated world. Too many activities are distractions demanding our attention, but so few activities really warrant the time and attention people give to them.

In my early twenties, I was on a hamster wheel, big time! I remember my friend Traci, a seasoned wife and mother, gifting me a book called *Having a Mary Heart in a Martha World*. The premise of this book was based on words of counsel to Martha, the organized and well-intended but wrongly-focused sister of Mary, who took pleasure in being still, being present, and listening. Martha complained of the work she was doing and how Mary should be doing more to help her with the responsibilities. Mary focused on the priority in the present moment, which Martha neglected in her efforts to get more done.

Tell me where your time, talent, and treasure are invested and I'll tell you where your priorities lie.

I totally related to Martha, because I lived in the 'do more, do it faster, do it better' lane in the early years of my adult life. To this day, I remind myself to assess between the critical and the urgent. I am mindful to think about what has my attention and what I am actually thinking about.

Our sensory-loaded minds can be indulged to the point of excess, which ultimately creates a lack of peace and stillness in some and is accompanied by physical and mental exhaustion for others. People have acclimated their lives to things that have no lasting benefit or substance. Some glorify overworking or demanding what they ask for...and they want it now! Some believe there is no need to have balance or priorities when we can do it all, be it all, and have it all, but I believe that narrative is a lie.

People are not meant to operate on all cylinders all the time, not even most of the time. It is a recipe for psychological, social, and relational breakdown. Women, many mothers in particular, have conditioned their bodies and minds to do more at home or work while giving less self-care, and it comes at a cost. The bill comes due at some point and the price is paid individually, and collectively, as a family and a society.

Let's go deeper. Our appetites can be insatiable when they are fed continually. We have appointments on our calendars and instant access via credit cards, Apple Pay, and cash apps. We stream what we want because it's all 'on demand.' Appetites become accustomed to what we eat; they can evolve into a never-ending, time-stealing, emotionally-draining rat race.

The main thing is what you crave, and it should not be a mystery to you. Tell me where your time, talent, and treasure are invested and I'll tell you where your priorities lie. What you pursue is the priority and the priority that gets the best of your time, talent, and treasure is your main thing.

The fitness guru who spends hours in the gym but has no time for school performances, and the corporate executive who is always traveling and rarely home – both have a main thing. The churchgoer who gives to the community but does not minister to their own family, and the artist who spends every free moment mastering their craft – they have found their main thing. While none of these activities are inherently wrong, a lack of prioritization can make them inherently problematic unless they are properly aligned in life.

People have an ideal self that is presented to others, but there's a private self that includes the thoughts, actions, and words we don't want advertised. Like the Johari window, we all have blind spots. Usually, these are not what we post comments about on social media, because they may not align with our self-image or what we want others to believe about us. It is common to judge others based on ideals and then relax our standards when it comes to looking at ourselves and being accountable for our words, actions, and decisions. Some people simply refuse to accept responsibility for their lifestyles, or the consequences that result from their choices.

Whether people accept it or not, there are consequences and unintended outcomes when priorities are misaligned. Do you have friends or associates who insist on getting together soon, but never have time to actually get together? For five years, they might repeat "Let's get together soon," but never make one effort to do so. This pattern speaks to priorities, and being comfortable with saying something while knowing it's not their priority or one they may never intend to follow through on.

Guardrails and balance are necessary to maintain proper priorities and a healthy life. Only in quiet reflection are our minds decluttered from the stress of just living. Simply living each day with the competing priorities and demands of a fast-paced society is enough to take a toll on the mind and body. Without practicing the art of being still and developing quietness of soul, we can diminish our capacity to handle the stress and adversities that come with life. Sadly, we don't know that we don't know our lives may be slowly unraveling under this constant strain.

This draining lifestyle presents temptations to take parenting shortcuts, and there are a multitude of options to bypass parenting responsibilities. One can only walk in purpose by staying focused on one's priorities, but how can we do that unless we know what they are? Mothers and fathers teach priorities to children. In most cases, we reproduce after our own kind. Children who do not understand the value of stillness lack an awareness of inward clarity, calm, and confidence.

Consider the rising diagnoses of attention deficit hyperactivity disorder (ADHD) in boys. Families are battling these labels from physicians and teachers who cannot handle the classroom behaviors of young, oftentimes brilliant, little boys. According to Johns Hopkins University, there are three types of ADHD and estimates suggest about 4-12 percent of children struggle with this disorder. Male children are two to three times more likely than female children to have the impulsive/ hyperactive or combined (hyperactive and inattentive) type of ADHD.[ii] This trend is a formidable opponent for our young sons to face and the barrage of cellphones, internet, gaming, videos, and television does not help them. Our children cannot overcome these obstacles without adults who model the right priorities and teach them to be responsible for their decisions and actions.

People of all walks of life have gone on quests hoping to discover what continues to elude them – the main thing. They are uncertain of what they do not know, which makes them susceptible to what they do not understand. Consequently, they misalign their priorities and lose focus on their purpose. They do not acknowledge that their internal motivations, or the reasons to wake up each day, are the key to prioritizing their day. The main thing is what characterizes the type of lifestyle we live, the priorities we set, and the company we keep.

Regardless of our beliefs or ideals, the proof of what is truly important is discovered in our routine actions and decisions. If you want to know your main thing, research your bank accounts and calendars, identify where you invest your energy, and what you are willing to sacrifice. No matter who you are and how many material possessions you have, there are constraints on time and energy. Everyone must prioritize their lives if they want to maximize their potential. Only a few things are eternally significant. Be honest with you. Is your self-image misaligned with your deliberate choices? If so, be encouraged, because you can choose to realign them.

Our children are influenced by what is taught, or what was caught, from the earliest stages of life. We learn lessons through observations and experiences. The lessons of life, in and out of the classroom, surround us through access to world events. American society, like other nations, has become a time-starved culture, over-saturated with the laundry list of our 'to-do' activities. Consider the difference that minor adjustments could make to your life and the lives of your family, especially your children.

Daily, people are searching for some 'thing' to fill financial, emotional, relational, or spiritual voids. They buy cars, only to trade them in a year later. They pursue hobbies, only to give them up. They pour themselves into careers, only to come up empty. Why? They lack an understanding of their true priorities. Is there any role more demanding than a working mother? Before children, I was indoctrinated on what success looked like without me knowing it. It was the higher education, good salary, office job, and of course, a family or marriage would do, but when I became a mother, my priorities shifted.

Subconsciously, I began indoctrinating my son with the model for success, just like I'd been taught. The firstborn child takes the brunt of our parenting deficiencies; we don't know that we don't know what we're doing. Most parents gain wisdom through trial and error. It is no surprise that firstborn children typically have a structured and responsible personality type. Most parents drill it into them because we want them to be 'successful.' They believe the success hype of career, money, and material possessions or other pleasures will bring the security they desire, but it can be deceiving.

A culture of standards should be a priority to parents who want to model leadership for their children, especially if they expect to raise sons who lead others, particularly their families. As progressive as our global society becomes, I find there is still an intrinsic value that people maintain about husbands, fathers, and ultimately their sons being leaders in their homes and communities. I realize this is a less popular perspective today, but popularity does not define facts or truth. The responsibility falls to parents to set standards and proactively engage with their children.

I would be remiss not to acknowledge the heroic work of single parents. I know many single mothers, and some fathers, who I watch do amazing jobs with their sons, despite the struggle of being the sole parent. There is no level of gratitude that would equate to the honor due to single parents raising children, particularly mothers raising sons.

What a father, or father figure, brings to the parenting dynamic is distinct from what a mother provides. There are differences in function that should be recognized and respected. Men and women can bring unique perspectives to a child's development. I remember times when my husband had more peace in taking certain actions with our sons. Sensing my concern, Dave would look at me and say, "They'll be alright." I sensed he knew something about their journey in that moment that I could not fully comprehend as their mother, because I am not a man. These times demonstrated that both roles of mother and father are necessary and complementary in our children's developmental process.

By our actions, or inactions, we choose to perpetuate a false narrative of success derived from material gain, degrees, and quests for power. People pour their lives into cultivating a talent or skill as if that will make success an automatic inheritance, not realizing our children need to matriculate into adulthood to be fully productive citizens. Success and the values ascribed to it are learned, and the lessons must be applied to be effective. For example, how many times have we heard what happens to the overnight lotto winners? They are bankrupt within a few years. Have you watched the multi-millionaire entertainer fall apart publicly, sometimes to their demise? While this is not the story with all lottery winners or entertainers, it is with a number of individuals who are not guided properly in managing their talent, or who fail to heed the lessons that could have protected their success.

If parents allow a culture of superficiality to dominate our families' structure and influence our children's perception of reality, we are accountable. From virtual reality games to reality television to social media, there is no shortage of fillers that seek to satisfy individual longings in our children's growth process. It is no wonder people are perplexed, distressed, and unable to grapple with the competing pressures of their life priorities.

Fluid and transient standards do not provide stability for the next generation. I am befuddled at the low resiliency in some young people compared to the incredible resiliency found in their contemporaries. Although I know we have varying strengths and weaknesses, this is a societal phenomenon to me.

By virtue of my family environment, I learned some behaviors at an early age that cultivated grit and innovative thinking. Environment plays a major role in our development. For example, I never met a lazy farmer. Anyone growing up on a farm will tell you about the early morning chores before school and the work performed daily as a way of life. The same could be said of the urban child who works after school and may help to support the household. These same children, if raised in different situations, may not develop an appreciation for hard work and sacrifice for the greater good. It depends on parenting and the values taught to them.

Growing up, I understood I was responsible for my emotions and the behaviors that followed, even when I was upset. It never occurred to me that I should take a weapon into a public or professional area with intent to harm others. I never considered attacking innocent people because of personal troubles or ridicule. I had difficulties, like anyone else, but acts of violence were just not options based on my upbringing. Before the 'going postal' era, the concept of mass shootings at work, school, or places of worship were rare. Since that time, they have become all too frequent. Was it an inherited trait, my upbringing, or learned social consciousness that kept me from going postal? Who teaches children how to exercise self-control and pursue their purpose? Who is charged with passing on corporate knowledge and societal 'rules' to future generations so children learn to value and prioritize life? I guess that depends on who we ask, and I am asking you.

> *Talent will never be enough*
> *to raise men of standard;*
> *they must possess character.*

Do you know the authority you are given in raising sons? Mothers are our children's first teachers; we shape our sons' hearts and minds. I am not condemning or judging any person, least of all the faithful mothers. None of us can know with certainty the outcomes and decisions of our children, but we have an obligation to mold them within the limited amount of time given to us before they make their own choices with their own consequences. If your sons were negatively impacted by parenting choices and you carry the guilt of that burden, I say carry it no longer…there is hope. You are not condemned for not being the perfect mother – none of us are! We all fall short of mothering our sons in some way that they need us. We have let them down or disappointed them in great or small ways. Our missteps are a part of understanding our humanity and our need to depend on a source that is greater than us to do this marvelous work of raising sons. We need faith, hope, and community to make it work for their good.

If you are in a place where you desire to be reconciled with your children, or anyone you influence, I suggest humbling yourself and going after them. Humility is a great equalizer and bridge for reconnection and reconciliation. After all, we determine the legacy we leave to future generations, including our children and grandchildren. Aren't they our priority – our main thing? I encourage you to examine your life to see if there is evidence of your investment in others.

Talent will never be enough to raise men of standard; they must possess character. Philippians 2:5-7 states: "You must have the same attitude that Christ Jesus had. Though He was God, He did not think of equality with God as something to cling to. Instead, He gave up His divine privileges; He took the humble position of a slave and was born as a human being." Whether you believe in Jesus or not, this demonstration of humility from One who willingly gives up their privileges for the good of others is admirable. Where do you see this type of sacrificial leadership today? Parenting is a sacrificial art and this is the type of example I want my sons to witness so they can be courageous on their journey to becoming leaders for such a time as this.

Rites of Passage

CHAPTER 3

PASSAGE OF BECOMING

"The unexamined life is not worth living."

Socrates

Becoming a mother changed my life and perspective. Parenting changes the lives of so many people. Can you remember what you did before kids? A couple of decades into this journey and it gets a little hazy for me. Yet, I know I had a life before I became a mother. I was an athlete in multiple sports and a student scholar throughout my primary and high school years. I led my peers as class president and even shared in the honor of being college 'co-valedictorian.' I became a professional and military officer, completing my graduate degree and exploring personal interests. I also married my high-school sweetie.

I accomplished all of these things and more before I became a mother, and I hardly think of them now. Seeing my firstborn son and holding him in my arms changed me in more ways than I could fathom. In fact, I changed during my pregnancy, and not just physically. I had no comprehension of patience and what a labor of love looked like until I had my first, and challenging, pregnancy.

When I learned I was pregnant, morning, afternoon, *and* evening sickness kicked in for the entire gestation period, along with excessive weight gain and back pain. This process sparked something I did not know resided in me. It was going to take a different kind of tolerance and fortitude to get through it. I knew quitting during pregnancy was not possible for me. I loved this little person who was giving me so much pain. I wanted to fight through it all and defend this life I had never met because somehow, I knew this person growing inside of me. I could sense his moods and agitations in the womb. When he was born, I got a deeper revelation and confirmation of all that had taken place during his development. Now he's a young man, I still chuckle when I see my son exhibit those same traits I noticed way back then.

Life does not wait for us to get ready; we have to choose to be prepared.

There was no going back to the old me because becoming a mom changes everything. It turned me into someone that never existed before that moment. While I struggled with the physical aspects, I recognized it was as much an internal transition as it was physical. I experienced new waves of emotions knowing there was nothing that could completely prepare me for becoming a mother. Even my thoughts changed. My decisions factored in this new life I was charged to guard.

I thought Elijah was the most precious person in the world when I first saw him. Most mothers think so when they see their child for the first time, but I was right! Elijah was incredibly alert and peaceful at birth. His temperament was one of fun and exploration. I enjoyed watching him develop in those early years. He truly amazed me as I studied his movements and tracked his progress. Anything physical came naturally to Elijah. He crawled at five months, stood up at seven months, and walked by nine months. Once he started moving, parenting went to the next level.

Noooo, I wasn't ready!!

Life does not wait for us to get ready; we have to choose to be prepared. When I think of what Elijah has done over the course of his life, most of it has been in the realm of physical activities. He began soccer at age three. He played football for a season, then basketball. By the time he reached middle school, he was a top student in Tae Kwon Do, selected as a member of the elite demonstration team, and had earned first place in competitions. I could not believe he was breaking boards and performing kicks above his head. Where did that originate? Certainly not from his parents, but the best was yet to come. He had achievements in cross country and track, too. Interestingly, we did not know he could run distances competitively until high school. His only intent for running was to improve his conditioning for basketball. He just decided to go out for a run one day, and came back miles later. I had a 'Ferreira Gump.'

Elijah never ceased to surprise me with his ability to master physical activities, but his emotional state was a different story. Going through some of his developmental stages was one of the hardest challenges of my life. From the moment I dreamed of Elijah's conception, everything I did from that point forward, I had him in mind. I changed from a small car to a big truck to accommodate a growing family. I made wiser financial decisions so Elijah could attend college and remain debt-free. Our diets changed; we wanted to be healthier and live longer, productive lives to see our son and grandchildren grow up.

Now, it was important to me to be there in the moments of my son's life. In reality, I could not be there for all of them because I still had competing priorities. I knew what was important, but was I living like it was important? Being in the military, I traveled for work and was deployed during Operation Iraqi Freedom. I missed family birthdays, anniversaries, and holidays. There was a period when I missed every family member's birthday and our wedding anniversary for three consecutive years.

Wherever I was, whatever I had to do, I knew I was still a mom and that fact grounded me. It made me want to come home and be a mother. So, I transitioned from a successful career to reset my priorities on God and family, then everything else. My new approach changed my perspective, which changed my plans, which changed my actions. I was not making choices for me or based on my convenience. I was making tough calls in the present and thinking about the future. I did not get all my choices right. No human parent will claim they do if they are honest with themselves and their children. We all fall short of our own expectations as parents, a hundred times over. Nevertheless, something drives us to persist in our struggles.

We want our children to experience more than us, possess more than us, and become more than us. How is this being, doing, and having more communicated to them? I believe it is through teaching them about their identity and self-worth. I was stunned to learn my eldest son suffered adverse ramifications from my time away for work. Maybe I was naïve to think it could not happen to me or my family. I did not see any warning signs initially. He was a great student. He is honorable in his actions and generous in his giving. He enjoys serving others and looks out for the 'little guy.' He was very well-liked by the pediatrician and school teachers, and in general, an all-around great person to know… but things derailed.

I dealt with a son I did not recognize. I recall looking at him one day thinking, where is my son? I knew him from the womb but I could not see him, though he was standing in front of me. People are quick to refer to childhood phases like 'terrible twos' and 'teenage years' when children lose their minds, but we never spoke those words over Elijah. No doubt, there is a transformation that takes place during those seasons for children and their parents. It has become acceptable for teenagers to be out of order, as if this is supposed to happen, but these behaviors should not be normalized. At no point are children supposed to be rebellious or disrespectful towards authority, teenagers or not. I struggled through this season of my life, especially while juggling my role as a military leader who practiced 'good order and discipline.' However, my reality at home did not align with the truth I believed and I had to make a choice. Which narrative was I going to believe about my son?

Becoming a mother changed me. Being a mother of a teenager humbled me. I thought we had it together as parents. I mean, our son was doing good in everything. We frequently received compliments on his manners, academics, and character. He was well-liked by people of influence, yet he had a void. Something was missing for him and we did not know how to fill that void. A few years of parental trials, some counseling, and lots of patience, prayer, and forgiveness brought us to another place of understanding as mother and son. It's still not a perfect place, but perfection is not our goal. We found a place of unconditional love and compassion in spite of our differences.

Becoming a mother changed me. Being a mother of a teenager humbled me.

While our perspectives were miles apart at times, no one would be allowed to do my son harm under my watch. I was his mother and that would never change. What was it that held us during those turbulent years? It was my steadfast commitment to raising a son with uncompromising standards. If you were to look at our calendars, bank accounts, and engagements, you would see Elijah's name written all over them during his childhood. I do not recall one school event or extracurricular activity that my husband or I did not attend to support him. A lot of the time, both of us were present because we wanted our son to know he was worth it – our time, money, and energy. Elijah was our main thing and, as parents, it was our responsibility to provide stability, helping him to develop and become who he was created to be. We were committed to being his anchors because our sons will face a battle and they must be prepared to win.

Rites of Passage

CHAPTER 4

PASSAGE OF NAMING

"A good name is to be chosen rather than great riches, loving favor rather than silver and gold."

Proverbs 22:1 (NKJV)

Birthdays are times of celebration for most people, and it is especially wondrous on the actual day that babies are born. A child's entrance into the earth is as dramatic as life gets until their passage into eternity. For every mother who has toiled in childbirth, the moment of triumph arrives when the sweet cry of her newborn baby is heard. With tired arms outstretched, the long-anticipated wait is over! She can breathe now, literally – the baby is off her lungs. The proud mother exhales with a smile of relief and tears of joy at the embrace of her child. Along with the father, maybe other significant family members, all have been invited to share in this glorious moment. Shortly thereafter, the time comes for the parents to officially declare their child's legal name.

Typically, naming a child is a subject of discussion for months. Some parents choose to keep it a secret until the child is born or host baby reveal parties. Some take votes because they can't decide and others debate or brood over lists of boys' and girls' names until something sticks. Do we name him after relatives? Is there a family tradition, like all the kids' names start with the letter T? Do parents pray and ask God? Do they name their child in honor of a loved one who passed on? Maybe they get creative – blending names to produce something new and usually hard to pronounce.

There is so much that is unique in our diverse world but this principle stands: all of us are called something by someone. We all have a name!

However a child's name comes about, there is no denying there must be a name. We are all known by our names – legal names or nicknames. For most people, we live with our birth name or a derivative for the remainder of our lives. Have you considered how many documents will have your name attached? How many times you will be asked to speak your name? How many times you will sign your name? Have you considered all your name means to you and to those who had the privilege of naming you?

Our first name is a lifelong commitment, barring any extraordinary measures to change it. It also connects us to our identity, yet we have no voice or opinion in choosing our name at birth. Both my husband and I will tell you, we did not like our names growing up. David was such a common name and there was always more than one in his class. Sonya wasn't too popular but it seemed to have no significance. There was nothing special about it and it was hard to find on those souvenir key chains. I did not like it…until I learned the meaning of my name.

We have no veto rights in our naming process. We get the name our parents or guardians give us. Decisions made about our name happen before we take our first breath. One of the most significant ceremonies in our lives will be our naming ceremony. It is a monumental event. Whether it is simple or extravagant, every child born on this earth receives a name, but why? What is in a name? What would be taken away and how would your life be different without a name? In part, that is what this book is all about – understanding certain rites of passage that form the foundation of individuality, familial relationships, and our cultural connection from generation to generation.

No matter the ethnicity, socioeconomic status, educational level, geographic location, or occupation, there is a naming process for children, sometimes more than one process. There is so much that is unique in our diverse world but this principle stands: all of us are called something by someone. We all have a name!

I believe children are a gift. One response to the blessing of being a parent is to identify and honor the child by bestowing a name. Some parents choose creative names and others are more traditional with naming. There is no right or wrong naming process, but there should be purpose in the chosen name. Since God gives gifts with a purpose, our children, being gifts, should be named with a purpose. Every child should know and understand their name from the beginning. Both of my children knew the meaning and spiritual connotations of their names from the time they could speak. Naming is one area we got right in our parenting decisions. While they do not have a full understanding of their names' power, they know their names identify them and their purpose is to walk in the authority that comes with their names.

My family did not provide any understanding of the importance of my name; they did not have the same revelation I do now. I do not know how they came up with my name and I had to discover what it meant. My husband had a similar experience. He was the only son in his family who had a biblical name. Imagine our amazement in adulthood when we discovered how accurately our names fit our lives.

In Hebrew culture, names were extremely important. Most sons were identified by their first name followed by 'bar,' meaning 'son of,' to denote belonging to a specific household. Are names powerful enough to shape our lives or are we transformed into the names we were given? I cannot say for certain, but words have meaning and power. I believe there is validity in both views. For example, Jacob means 'deceiver' and with guidance from his mother, he lived up to his name by deceiving his father and stealing from his brother. After Jacob encountered God, his name was changed to Israel, which means 'struggles or wrestles with God.' Jacob knew he needed to change, and God has a way of calling out the potential in us. Even when we do not know who we are, God knows who He created us to be and that is the person He calls out in each of us.

As parents, we are communicating a message to and about our sons when they are named. Their names designate ownership and create a sense of belonging. Our sons need to know they have a place of belonging in this world. They are not an accident or mistake. It is an error to name our children based on temporary situations instead of calling out their future potential and value. Names mean something and should reflect purpose.

In the case of the Pharisee Saul (name meaning 'ask for'), he is renamed Paul (small). I believe it was necessary for him to be renamed, because Saul lived a self-righteous and violent life. After encountering Jesus, he had a stark transformation in his character and identified with his value to God. Now he required a new name that aligned with his purpose and reflected the humility shown in his zealous service to God and others.

So, what does your name communicate about you and your children? A message is being heralded to the world on every document they sign so it is critical as mothers we call forth the leaders, the men we want our sons to be, and it starts with their names.

CHAPTER 5
PASSAGE OF TRADITIONS AND CEREMONIES

"Beware the man of a single book. We must love them both, those whose opinions we share and those whose opinions we reject, for both have labored in the search for truth, and both have helped us in finding it."

Saint Thomas Aquinas

We have all kinds of ceremonies today, from weddings to graduations to memorials. In some ways, we function as a ritualistic society. People develop routines that may allow them to fall into the trap of going through the motions because 'that's what we do.' If we get lost in the mundane, we can lose the significance of the moment.

Our time as parents goes by quickly, so we should be astute and recognize the value of special occasions that memorialize the milestones for our children. Time is a finite commodity, a precious gift and effective parenting helps us invest in the success of future generations.

In 2017, I was serving in my final military assignment, so I was traveling for work frequently and spent my last tour across the country, separated from my family. During this season, I got the idea to honor my eldest son, Elijah, for his 16th birthday, but it was destined to be more than just a gathering. Elijah would have a rite of passage ceremony. The purpose of this ceremony was to provide him with guidance and support to transition into the next season. Every detail was contemplated, from the meaning of the event to those selected to participate. We had one issue: how were we going to explain something we'd never seen before to people who didn't know what a rite of passage ceremony entailed? Better yet, how would we convince them it was worth their time and money to partake in this momentous occasion?

I knew taking on this event would be a challenge for me because I did not grow up with elaborate birthday celebrations, much less a ceremony. I confess, birthday gatherings were not significant in my childhood. In fact, I only recall having one birthday party, and not actually the party, just the birthday cake that I snuck into the kitchen to see on the counter. I do not recall what else happened that day or any other birthday celebrations. It just wasn't our family 'thing.'

I went through life without thinking much about my birthday. Sure, I would wish people happy birthday, but I did not really understand the reason people placed such importance on having a celebration. Why not just give thanks for being alive, without all the hoopla? From my point of view, I was truly blessed if anyone besides my husband and my mom thought of me for my birthday. I had no expectations for celebrating my life in that way and that was fine with me. I do not blame anyone for my choices or attitude towards birthdays. I understand they are special days to some people, but I perceived them differently.

However, over the years, I learned birthdays have meaning and significance, and should be recognized in some way. While I continue to keep a low profile, I enjoy celebrating others' birthdays much more because it is meaningful to them. As life would have it, my 'birthday epiphany' was a timely blessing because our second son, Ephraim, is enthralled with his birthday. He would start planning his next birthday party the day after his birthday party. We did all kinds of activities to remind him how special he was to us because he believes his birthday is special. Actually, he believes it is a national holiday, and expects everyone to get the memo to celebrate him throughout the month of August.

As it happened, Ephraim's birthday is the day before mine. Coincidence, I think not! So, every year since his arrival, I have no choice but to get excited for our birthdays, more so his celebration of both of our birthdays. Fortunately, I do not mind being overshadowed by Ephraim's youthful exuberance and none of his birthdays lacked celebration and fanfare. Nothing was too over-the-top for Ephraim.

Since his conception and birth were miraculous to me, he is worth celebrating. Every day of his life has proven that fact. I believe this is true about every child, especially those children whose mothers had to endure extreme difficulties in conception, pregnancy, and labor. I experienced severe complications during my pregnancy with Ephraim, beyond the extreme morning sickness I dreaded with my first pregnancy. The challenges and defeats in this process made me love Ephraim all the more for his tenacious spirit and spunk, even in the womb. He is cherished and celebrated, in part, because of the circumstances that surrounded his arrival. I know we are blessed to have him. In mothering him, I have to remind myself of that blessing regularly when I am tempted to be frustrated by his tenacious spirit manifesting in his strong will and persistent personality.

When I reflected on how we celebrated Ephraim, I realized I did not have the same intentionality with my eldest son. Of course, Elijah had birthday parties and we celebrated him too, but our focus (and our financial means) were different at that time. Since our sons are 10 years apart, we had the benefit of learning a lot of parenting lessons before Ephraim arrived. So, when Elijah was preparing to turn 16, I got a revelation that he needed to be honored in a special way. I believe I was given a specific vision of how to honor him as a son on the precipice of manhood. In faith, our family began the journey of building the rites of passage with his birthday ceremony.

Through revelation, I understood these family moments were more than food, fun, and fellowship, although there's no Ferreira celebration without those things being considered. I had to process some questions: What is a rite of passage ceremony? Really, what does it look like? What does it mean? I had no practical context in my life and no clue how to make it happen, since these ceremonies were not performed during my upbringing. Thankfully, my worldview keeps expanding to encompass more experiences that take me to deeper places of love and fellowship.

I prayed, meditated, and researched rites of passage until it occurred to me that even babies have to go through a rite of 'passage' from the beginning. In natural childbirth, babies enter the world by a passageway or canal. This thought made me ponder my family, my cultural experiences, and my interactions with others. I found no personal connection to a rite of passage ceremony, but I did not let that stop me.

In the planning phase, I wondered, when does a boy become a man and does he know it? Is it when he gets a driver's license, graduates high school and/or college, gets the first 'real' job, moves out of his parents' house, or pays his own cellphone bill (definitely a step in the right direction)? Maybe it is when he gets married and becomes a parent. Life is not a mathematical equation, so everyone's journey is different. Considering these things illustrated a pattern in which children in America are conditioned to think about their transitions into the next stage of life.

Then I began thinking on what God said about children, particularly sons, transitioning into adulthood. In 1 Corinthians 13:11, it states: "When I was a child, I spoke as a child, I understood as a child, thought as a child; but when I became a man, I put away childish things." The principle of maturation in this verse can apply to anyone, but I am focusing on the transition from boyhood to manhood. This verse was intriguing to me because it indicates that a successful transition into adulthood requires a specific action. It is critical to put away childish things in order to become a man.

As I mused over these words, it prompted more questions for me as a mother, like how does a boy know when he has put away childish things and cross into manhood? Who confirms the transition in the boy's life? This is a path he has not taken before, so how could he know unless someone shows him? I wondered if most men have clear responses to these questions. Do they even think about this process, or do they just stumble into it without regard? Even men I talk to who've obtained independence and some measure of success in life seem to be unsure of the answers to these questions. My sons, your sons, deserve more support and confirmation in their matriculation process.

It is critical to put away childish things in order to become a man.

American culture tends to rush growing up at the same time as it hinders maturing for young men. In the past generation, between the 1970s and 2020s, America created a different set of cultural values, norms, and tolerances than previously practiced. It has evolved on a national stage and repeating "one nation under God, indivisible, with liberty and justice for all" almost sounds cliché. Historically, America was not founded on liberty or justice for all people and it has never fulfilled the promise of being one nation of equal opportunity for everyone. America has potential and has progressed in some areas so I don't believe the ideology of being unified as a nation is something to dismiss. We need unity to survive. Sadly, America is still separated by our differences and a lack of empathy towards others. Even within our own self-identifying groups of ethnicity, religion, or gender, we have factions – we remain divided.

America is not the only nation that has traversed this divisive territory. Bigotry, division, and hatred play out on the international stage as well. I am reminded of the words stated in 2 Chronicles 7:13-14: "At times I might shut up the heavens so that no rain falls, or command grasshoppers to devour your crops, or plagues among you. Then if My people who are called by My name will humble themselves and pray and seek My face and turn from their wicked ways, I will hear from heaven and will forgive their sins and restore their land." In this verse, God is speaking to believers, not a general audience. He is telling those who profess to have an intimate relationship with Yahweh and see aspects of our world falling apart from natural disasters and plagues of every kind, including social plagues like racism, sexism, pornography, and human trafficking, prayer should be their response for healing and uniting people – we must pray!

Once believers get up from praying, a question remains: are we acting in accordance with our prayer? This instruction is only to those who have the ears to hear the voice of God, as believers have done for centuries, to help their nations be restored. When something is broken, it needs mending. Our world has a lot of brokenness. Healing is available to nations but it comes with this condition: believers must be the ones to humble themselves and pray. The people of God must seek His wisdom and turn their hearts, with corresponding actions, back to righteousness. Only then will God listen and respond by healing the land.

In biblical times, the children of Israel called for days of national fasting when they were facing calamity or threats of destruction from their enemies. They established a pattern of falling away from God, being subjected to oppression, seeking God for deliverance, and then being restored only to repeat. The celebration of Purim is a commemoration of the Jewish people's deliverance from genocide during their exile in the Persian empire. The story unfolds in the Book of Esther 3:5-13 with a sly motive set against the Jewish people. In this story, a wicked plot to destroy all Jews was uncovered but Queen Esther was willing to approach her husband the King of Persia, on behalf of her people, the Jewish people. Before she took this life-and-death risk, she declared a time of national fasting and prayer for the entire nation of Israel to seek and hear from God. This story of the Jews' salvation from entrenched racial hatred in high places and planned genocide is accompanied by prayer.

Israel is one of the smallest countries in the Middle Eastern region and it is surrounded by adversaries. The Jewish nation has been attacked, the people persecuted, and subjected to exile yet the nation of Israel is still standing. Judaism teaches the importance of knowing one's spiritual identity and cultural history as the people of Yahweh. Foundational spiritual beliefs are passed down generationally in Jewish families. Their rites of passage serve as a channel to galvanize them as a family, community, culture, and nation.

Indigenous and tribal cultures appear to be more in tune with the value of recognizing their sons in rites of passage ceremonies. Their survival and tribal way of life may depend upon their ability to raise men, and sometimes women warriors, to be leaders and protectors of their communities. The common thread in these cultures is that all members are expected to contribute to the collective good, so it is vital to set expectations and standards for becoming productive men in their society. If one eats, they all eat; therefore, helping the next generation is not only beneficial but a requirement for them to live as a community. There seems to be a greater sense of working together within the tribal family and village. Young men learn from older men. Older women teach younger women. Together, their society thrives. Contemporary society should learn from this example.

I like to watch documentaries. I watched some depicting the way tribal villagers and indigenous people interacted with one another in their communities, beyond the superficial lines of 'that's my family by blood.' They understood each member along with their uniqueness and cultivated their value and self-esteem. This type of daily life teaching appeared to be a passage for their children to follow in 'the way' while becoming who they were meant to be. The adults in these communities actively and intentionally called out the greatest parts of their children when interacting with them. If a father expected his sons to be great hunters, fishermen, or farmers, he told them so and they believed they could do it.

In the storytelling, the father is not abrasive but loving, respectful, and encouraging of his sons' development, and not just that of his sons but the community. It is no ordinary task for children to herd flocks in mountains, gather water in buckets from springs miles away, or provide game for the family to eat, but these tribal children learned to do so. They are not spoiled or pampered when it comes to their survival and that of their people, because their village's survival depends on the childrens' development.

I was amazed by what the children are taught and expected to learn at young ages by modern standards. In my suburban neighborhood, mothers struggle to let our sons walk to the bus stop alone, or even stay there with a group of friends without hovering. In contrast, these young boys are in the wild and learning how to become hunters and productive men of their society before the age of ten. Astonishing, and it got me pondering: am I underestimating my sons' capacity and calling out the greatest part of them? Children should be spoken to with the intention of calling out who they are becoming, not how they behave or who they are at present.

In some cultures, when young boys or girls are entering adulthood, there are rites, traditions, and ceremonies they participate in to be accepted as men and women of the community. Families of Latin American descent may celebrate with a Quinceañera, a time of honoring a young Latina girl who comes of age. Although I have not participated in this ceremony, I have seen the planning and preparation that can go into this occasion. The investment into this rite of passage is significant for some, although it varies by family. It is no small designation to be honored at the Quinceañera, which oftentimes includes taking holy communion along with other familial or cultural traditions. The young girl is being honored, but the entire family and community are celebrating this milestone and her passage into womanhood.

People of the Jewish community perform bar mitzvahs and bat mitzvahs. These ceremonies acknowledge a young boy or girl transitioning from childhood to adulthood. It is a time when they become responsible for understanding and practicing Judaism; they become accountable for their own actions. These rites of passage normally happen around the ages of 12 or 13 years old. At an age where most American parents would consider their middle-school child just a child, the Jewish community is rallying around their sons and daughters to help them understand how to become men and women.

It takes grit to transition into adulthood. Grit is personal fortitude developed in a crucible and without it, no one can excel. I would not have the resilience required to raise my sons without grit. Being a parent takes perserverance and it is by far the most taxing responsibility a person can have, if they are engaged. It fires from all directions, consistently and with little reprieve. Proper parenting motivates our children to grow and overcome barriers to their progress in academia, corporate industry, the military, or any other profession

When I finally got my Air Force commission, it was like starting over in middle school because I had similar cultural experiences in my work environment as the only person of color, or the only female, or the only female of color, take your pick. In those particular leadership positions, I grew accustomed to offhand comments and not feeling like I fit in with peers because I had a unique perspective and different experiences that they could not, or maybe did not desire, to understand. I was, at times, an outsider in my own community of military brothers and sisters because my peers did not relate to me outside of their own filters.

This is not to say I didn't agree with my leadership or peers; I did, many times. However, by listening to others' perspectives, they could have gained a broader view of the issues at hand and the impact on a diverse workforce. I was blessed with some leaders who understood me and welcomed my contributions to the organization. When I encountered leaders who did not welcome me, I was well-equipped in my response based on past experiences.

From the age of 12, being different was a recurring theme to me, as if I was being asked, "Why are you sitting at this table and how did you get here?" I still hear piercing echoes of that theme in some circles. Most leaders today do not want to be perceived as 'intolerant' of differences, so they present as inclusive or caring. For a long time, people of color and women, or those not in the majority group, were 'tolerated,' not accepted for their talents, technical expertise, or cognitive diversity.

Still, children of color face similar difficulties because they perceive the world and reason differently in an educational system designed for standardization; it leaves little room for diverse thinking or innovation.

One of my favorite scriptures refers to safety by seeking wise counsel from people who can cover my blind spots. We all have them. In practice, this means I have to rely on people who see situations differently than I do and I need to leverage their inputs to make sound leadership decisions. I applied this principle so often in my approach to leading, including adapting my own welcome speech when I assumed a new leadership role.

In my first leadership meeting, I explained, "All of us will make mistakes, including me, but we are a team. I believe I am surrounded by experts to give me strategic guidance so I can navigate the complexities of leading a diverse group of people within our organization. I am open to hearing your thoughts and proposed solutions to problems, because I may like your ideas better than mine. I know we will not always agree on my decisions, but that is to be expected. Different perspectives are welcomed because they sharpen our thinking, as long as we maintain respect." Finally, I would close out by saying, "If you agree with me on every decision, you will be the first person to do so and I will be suspicious." That introduction never failed to get a laugh and establish a great rapport with key members of my team. In return, I felt their loyalty and support even when they disagreed with my decisions, because they assumed noble intent and trusted my motives.

This same principle of embracing diversity applies to other social dynamics, including parents' authority and leadership styles in their homes. Our children are not life experts, for sure, but they can give us insight into their thoughts, dreams, plans, and emotions if we listen. I read a great quote from Andy Stanley: "Leaders who do not listen will be surrounded by people who have nothing to say." I surmise from his quote: "Parents who do not listen will be surrounded by children who have nothing to say." My personal experiences show that leaders who have to be right and have it their way, and refuse to adapt or take advice, have quiet meetings. The room is filled with silence from people who no longer have a desire to innovate or share ideas, or feel safe enough to disagree. Unfortunately, this same ineffective communication happens in our homes.

If agreement was the standard for conversation, almost no one would talk!

I disagree with my sons on various matters, but that does not mean they should not be heard as long as we can speak respectfully. We need to practice the art of disagreement with civility instead of being disagreeable. Civility in discourse is becoming a lost art and parents need to revive it for children who are to become leaders. I know my sons believe I did not listen to them when I didn't agree, but agreement is not required for people to listen and dialogue about different views, ideas, and dreams. If agreement was the standard for conversation, almost no one would talk! Rather, let empathy, and considering the perspective of others to be as equally important as our own, engulf our communication so we intentionally close the gaps, correct disparities, and grow through differences. There could be more common ground than most people realize when opposing parties, including parents and children, listen to understand and not to defend their views.

We should consider how societies of the past flourished for long periods of time. What did they do right, and what was their downfall? For millennia, various cultures celebrated their children's transition into adulthood. America, not so much. In his book, *Raising a Modern-Day Knight*, Robert Lewis describes ceremonies as the "crown jewel" to help a boy become a man. He writes: "In many cultures throughout history, a teenage boy is taken through some type of ritual to mark his official passage into manhood. I believe one of the greatest tragedies in Western culture is the absence of this type of ceremony."[iii] I agree with his conclusion.

America is a younger nation formed of diverse cultural groups. American ancestry is a compilation of indigenous people, enslaved Africans, and immigrants from around the world. Our families and cultural traditions come mostly from our ancestral heritage, which includes but is not defined by one type of American view. We are Americans because of our shared beliefs, values, and traditions that make us unique as a nation. These traits are passed on and influence our society generationally. For example, many Catholics can speak to the significance of their first communion. Members of the Muslim community can share the importance of their pilgrimage and times of prayer. In the Mormon community, there is a focus on missions and service to those in need. Jehovah's Witnesses have a strong foundation in evangelism. All of these traits are learned, typically in a family or community.

While I may differ in my spiritual beliefs and customs, I respect their right to their beliefs even if I don't espouse them, because free people should have freedom to choose. Since we live in a diverse world, some differences may never be resolved, but it is critical to understand one another and extend grace in order to have a healthy society that can function for the good of its members.

Our expressed differences create the 'mixed salad' of American culture, and much of American tradition is borrowed and not exclusive to America. America integrated the language, customs, and ancestral heritage of various cultures and nations to build this country, so we should learn to live with some measure of harmony among each other. What do I mean? There are holidays that are celebrated globally across cultural or religious boundaries, like Christmas. There are also holidays associated with a particular group of people, such as Passover or Ramadan. Then there are holidays like Juneteenth and July Fourth that are specific to America. Even with these American holidays, they can be divided within the American culture. Not all Americans acknowledge Kwanzaa or Indigenous Peoples' Day, but some do.

In our different expressions, we need not be divisive because there are still shared American values. For example, Kwanzaa is an African-American cultural holiday rooted in Swahili traditions. It was created in 1966 by Dr. Maulana Karenga for the purpose of celebrating seven principles that focused on living in a community, working for the collective good, and serving others. The seven Kwanzaa principles are unity, self-determination, collective responsibility, cooperative work and economics, purpose, creativity, and faith. While Kwanzaa is a time to honor African-American culture and ancestry, these same principles are incorporated within the larger American culture as well. We cannot be "one nation under God, indivisible" without unity (Umoja), purpose (Nia), and faith (Imani), the same principles espoused in Kwanzaa. These unifying principles are embedded in the fabric of America; they cannot be removed without destroying the very fabric of the foundation itself.

My family recognizes Kwanzaa principles because it reminds us of the greater good and our responsibility to give back or contribute to the communities in which we work and live. It also reinforces a parental responsibility to think about our family from a generational perspective, along with the obligation to care about the collective society surrounding us. It reminds me to have compassion for neighbors, especially the sick or elderly. Kwanzaa is more than an African-American cultural holiday to me; it is an American holiday teaching principles that most parents hope their children will embrace.

I reflected on my most recent review of the Preamble to the United States Constitution and the Preamble of the Declaration of Independence.[1] While the historical context of these documents was exclusive towards enslaved Blacks and women, I do not believe a poorly executed vision means the vision was all bad. As the saying goes, let's not throw the baby out with the bath water. American slavery and all its kindred, like the Black Codes and Jim Crow, were an evil plague and, sadly, their remnants remain. Unfortunately, an oppressive spirit still exists in different guises and mindsets that contribute to a growing fault line between diverse groups of people in American society. Some agree that

[1] - SEE PREAMBLES ON PAGE 64

57

the Constitution and Declaration of Independence were masterfully written documents, but America has not lived up to their promises. This failure of leadership delivery results in disillusion with these documents, but I contend that does not have to be the case. The baby is worth saving, even if the bath water is filthy.

Who can say they have not felt the impact of increased racial tension, cries for social justice, and even ethnic or gender violence globally? The re-emergence of generational strife and ethnic division in America has been a sobering reminder of a repeated pattern of how far we have not come in making good on the opportunity for all to share in the 'American dream.' Our children and future generations inherit the unfinished business of the country. The same cultural issues will continue to fester unless we decide a change starts with us. If we want to preserve human dignity, establish communication across our differences, and move toward a more unified nation, then we'd better start doing something to make that happen within our own sphere of influence, beginning at home. What are we teaching our children? What are we demonstrating or saying privately about other groups of people? Are we fostering a climate that contributes to misunderstanding and poor behaviors in our society, or helping create solutions? By nurturing sons to be men of integrity and character, I believe mothers are contributing to the solution.

When I was younger, there was a popular children's show called *Schoolhouse Rock*. It was an educational program with an ingenious way to capture young minds by stimulating their creativity to learn math, science, grammar, and history through music. One of the most popular songs from this program is called "Three is a Magic Number." It was a fun song to sing, but being enlightened, I know three is not a magic number, and neither is 18.

The majority of young men are not prepared for manhood at 18 years old, and parents know their sons still need nurturing and guidance at this age.

American society treats 18 years of age as the golden standard for maturity. At 18, we become legal adults who can register to vote, sign binding contracts, enter military service, and are no longer considered 'minors' in need of parental consent. In some cases, parents dismiss their children from the household, whether their sons are mentally and emotionally prepared for it or not. Why – because they are legal adults at 18. But are they men?

The majority of young men are not prepared for manhood at 18 years old, and parents know their sons still need nurturing and guidance at this age. We know this to be true because we've been 18 before, and there remains significant life matters that most young adults cannot handle effectively on their own. So, parents, why do we buy into this narrative of the 'magical 18 years old as being an age when children need to "get out my house" when we have not cultivated a society for young men to be fully independent and successful at 18 years old? They are not equipped with enough leadership tools or experiences to lead themselves, much less families and communities.

By that age, most young adults have not settled into their own identity, purpose, or place in society. How can they be expected to lead others when they are still finding their way? In other cases, mothers coddle their sons to the point of codependency long past 18 years of age because they cannot stop seeing them as just 'my babies' instead of the leaders they are intended to be. These adult 'babies' still require their parents' support for healthcare, college tuition, and car insurance. Some take decades after college to move out of their parents' house and some never leave, or leave and return. I have talked with mothers who are paying their sons' car insurance and cellphone bills well after they graduate college, get married, and begin their own families. Still think 18 is a magic number?

In other cultures, milestones are celebrated with the passing of responsibility for oneself, not just time, and there are obligations to be productive citizens contributing to their communities. America, we have been hoodwinked and bamboozled into acting like chronological age equates to developmental maturity. It certainly does not! The evidence of this can be found in American households with grown children, and it is the reason that a rite of passage ceremony should be honored as a capstone moment necessary to help our young men understand their role in the family and greater society.

As a mom, it was a gift to understand early that my sons do not belong solely to me. They are on loan to me from

God, and I am a steward. I am accountable for their well-being and consider myself the 'Chief Steward' of God's precious gifts to me. By living with the end goal in mind, I knew that at some point I would not be my sons' leading lady in life. My sons will fall in love and find women to capture their hearts. I must be okay with that fact because it is the natural order of things. Children grow up; they enter adult relationships and grow their own families. Don't get me wrong; I expect my sons to always honor and respect their parents. I will set them straight if they cross the respect line. However, for them to be men of standard, my sons will have to embrace their positions as leaders, husbands, and father figures, which take priority over their roles as my sons.

My friends, it is a requirement to let go of the reins holding on to our adult sons. Let them be men and, as mature mothers, let us avoid contentions with their spouses. Mothers must allow their sons' wives to take their proper positions in their lives. It is hard for a new husband to balance the roles of son to his mother and husband to his bride when there is strife between them. Mothers should not compete with their sons' love interests. It is a maternal responsibility to defer at the appropriate time and ease our son's transition into being a married man. This shift in familial order is a huge rite of passage and, if done properly, brings not only honor but also joy to mothers, knowing their investment was not in vain.

In some marriages, the mothers of sons are at war with their daughters-in-law, and this should not be. In an ever-changing society with shifting values and identities, I consider it a blessing to raise sons who desire to marry, raise their own children, and lead their own families. Between 1998 and 2021, the median age for American males to marry has steadily increased, reaching 30 years old for the first marriage.[iv] Other nations are seeing similar trends, with even higher median ages in places like the United Kingdom. The census data for 2021 reveals the average age of males choosing marriage for the first time in England and Wales was just over 34 years old in 2019 and the number of opposite-sex marriages has consistently decreased, falling by 50 percent since 1972.[v]

In contemporary societies, research shows the average age at which males choose marriage is increasing, and I wonder what this data is telling us about the value of marriage and family in modern societies. What are mothers teaching and modeling for our sons about transitioning into husbands and fathers who lead their families and build stability in their communities? Based on economic and personal desires, men and women choose to delay entering a marriage covenant for longer, and some never do, even though they desire to have intimate, fulfilling, and committed sexual relationships. The effects of not showing our sons how to be productive adults and loyal men delay their ability to embrace life transitions, which may stunt their emotional development and undermine their confidence to be men, husbands, and fathers.

Our sons are screaming for validation in these areas because it does not happen automatically when they turn 18 years old. The type of validation they need is built over time through successes and failing forward at each stage of life. There are no shortcuts. Every son must matriculate, or he will be inept to lead and may struggle with feelings of inadequacy throughout his lifetime. For the sake of our families and communities, this cannot be. It is no accident that a son who properly honors and loves his mother tends to honor and love his wife. Mothers, let it be our custom to lean into the rite of passage for our sons as they take on adulthood and responsibilities for themselves, their families, and leading in society.

PREAMBLE OF THE DECLARATION OF INDEPENDENCE
(ADOPTED - JULY 4, 1776)

We hold these truths to be self-evident, that all men are created equal, that they are endowed by their Creator with certain unalienable Rights, that among these are Life, Liberty and the pursuit of Happiness.

PREAMBLE OF THE CONSTITUTION OF THE UNITED STATES
(RATIFIED – JUNE 21, 1788)

We the People of the United States, in Order to form a more perfect Union, establish Justice, insure domestic Tranquility, provide for the common defense, promote the general Welfare, and secure the Blessings of Liberty to ourselves and our Posterity, do ordain and establish this Constitution for the United States of America.

In view of these principles, our children deserve our best efforts to pass down an inheritance of justice, freedom, and equality. We may never arrive at the zenith of these iconic principles but in our pursuit of them we will become better mothers, fathers, and citizens.

My Passage

"Start where you are, use what you have, and do what you can."

Arthur Ashe

I remember being a responsible child when I was growing up. By age 12, I had chores and cleaned up my mess. I got myself up and ready for school or the activities of the day. I practiced my Christian faith by studying the Bible and memorizing verses. I was emerging as a leader of my peers at school, even though secretly I struggled with fledgling confidence and mediocre self-esteem; however, I worked hard and excelled in academics. It was during this time that I had two very special seventh-grade teachers from Esperanza Middle School take an interest in me: one a language arts teacher, Mr. J. Dobson, and my math teacher, Mr. M. Sweeney.

With the racial and cultural division in America today, I believe it is important to note that both teachers were White males and they played a unique place in my academic achievements, such that I continued to visit them at the school long after I departed. It is my personal experience that a teacher or leader does not have to be of the same ethnicity or background to make a huge impact on children. They simply have to care enough to do so. However, that does not mean understanding a student's ethnicity, unique perceptions, or cultural experiences is irrelevant to learning. These are critical factors in educational environments and are sometimes used as barriers in academic systems.

Mr. Dobson's and Mr. Sweeney's ability to teach with passion enabled them to see their work as more than a job or a paycheck. They believed in learning and they believed every student could learn. Although I never believed I was simple-minded, they were the first teachers to make me believe I was more intelligent than I thought. They activated my vision to see I had more to offer. It was through their encouragement that I began pushing past predetermined societal barriers based on gender, race, disability, socioeconomic status, and other stereotypes about who I was and who I could become. Their willingness to reach out instead of overlook me changed the course of my life and consequently, the lives of many others I later touched. Indeed, this transition functioned as a rite of passage for me.

In my academic journey, I was set apart from my peers. None looked like me or related to my experiences except for one Filipina student, who became my only friend. I entered a new world where students were respected at school and were not only taught well, but were engaged in intellectual discourse with teachers and peers. Interestingly, they also 'acted out,' with different behaviors that were accepted in this learning environment that would not have been tolerated in other classrooms. I dared not take these classroom behaviors home with me, yet my exposure to this aspect of the primary school educational system unlocked my thinking. These experiences opened my mind to infinite possibilities. After all, isn't that the purpose of education – to increase our capacity to think, create, and envision?

After my encounters with Mr. Sweeney and Mr. Dobson, I discovered my academic abilities went far beyond the options presented to me. Since they believed in me, from that point forward, I was placed in accelerated classes with advanced coursework, with their aid. By the time I got to high school I was transcribing Latin scrolls, something I'd never considered doing before. My entire academic paradigm shifted about my place in this world and in American society. Where would I be if Mr. Dobson and Mr. Sweeney had not called something out of me? I believe those teachers were divine disruptors who broke the pattern and ushered me to another level. It was my personal rite of passage in discovering who I am and what I can contribute to my community and the world at large. At the ripe age of 12, without fanfare or ceremony, I took my place and started running my race in academics. I have not stopped running.

Despite economic disadvantages, something in me believed against the odds. This educational indoctrination awakened me, nurturing my pursuit of knowledge in my soul. I could not rest with just being average or getting by; excellence was the standard and that attitude was instilled in me at home and at school, from a very young age. There was a spirit of determination and hope of promise that called out to me from a place deep within.

Those teachers did not create that hope, but they were catalysts for my future. They were vessels who spoke life into my purpose. I sensed their support and pride in my accomplishments as they watched my development. I saw their concern when I fell short of expectations, and they did not hesitate to hold me accountable. I was more disappointed in myself if I disappointed them.

I also saw their compassionate eyes when I was rejected by my classmates, mostly because I did not fit in with them. My classmates did not empathize with my cultural situation, nor did they include me in their small group activities. In the lunchroom, I went back to friends from my cultural community, but I did not fit in well there either. I quickly realized there are places and boundaries where others just can't go with me because I was not on their path. Those times are lonely, difficult moments for young minds to process. All of these things had to happen for me to begin the journey of becoming me so I could be the best individual, leader, and mother for my sons. Looking back, I know these early trials were preparation for similar tests I would face when I became an Air Force officer and the mother of sons who are called to be set apart.

I was ready to receive what Mr. Dobson and Mr. Sweeney imparted to me only because I first sensed God shifting me to something new. The year prior, I was sitting in my sixth-grade language arts class, watching my teacher spit-shine her car keys. This was not the type of classroom that demonstrated care or excellence. She was a strange teacher, and even as I reminisce on her actions today, I wonder how stable she really was at that time. Students did not come to her class to learn. They behaved as they pleased, because education was not her priority either. I often sat in her class wondering, what is this all about? The classroom chaos created a level of tension and discomfort that made learning in that environment a challenge. As I surveyed the room, I saw other students I knew. A few lived in my neighborhood. Others I'd met at church or some community activity. We all had one thing in common: there was little demand placed on children from our community when it came to academics. We were not expected to thrive; we were merely there to survive if we were lucky.

As I looked around at my sixth-grade classroom environment, I heard a soft voice in my heart ask me one question: "What are you doing here?" Somehow, I immediately knew this was not a normal encounter. The voice spoke to my soul, my purpose, and my identity. When I 'heard' this question, something clicked inwardly and, in that moment, my trajectory was recalculated. I heard the question and sat up in my chair with my answer: "I don't belong here." It only took seconds for me to grasp the revelatory nature of this question from my Creator. He was reaching out directly to realign me with His purpose for my life.

Reflecting on the question "What are you doing here?" it seemed my heart already knew my future potential and responded to the 'voice' calling me upward. As I answered the call, I also settled the matter of my self-worth and purpose in my own heart. Our plans of action should be to get busy advancing in our purpose and discovering our place of possibilities. I did not know how to move in this new academic dimension. I knew even less how to do it without influence, charisma, or social status. At this time in my life, I would say I saw myself as a grasshopper in my own eyes, but I was beginning to unveil the inner giant.

One thing I love about God encounters is that once a person meets Him in earnest, there is no denying something happened, something changed.

My teachers saw beyond my circumstances and peered into my future. They told me what I could be when I could not see it on my own. Sometimes we need to ride the hope of another we trust until we have the wings to fly independently. I did not fully know I could do what they said, but I believed they believed I could do it and that was enough for me to get moving. With few tools in my belt, I had to figure out what skills I could cultivate into more opportunities for me. I knew I was a good student in elementary school, but I realized I was intelligent when I entered middle school. It is a good practice for parents to tell their children how smart they are, but it is another reality when their children believe it.

My academic performance resulted in a conference with my teachers, who asked me if I thought I was in the right classes. They asked me if I would be interested in trying more advanced curricula and challenging my academic rigor. No other student like me was moved into these advanced classes that year, but I accepted the challenge. I knew God had spoken to me and He was opening a door of opportunity that would ultimately break strongholds for my entire family, including my sons. One thing I love about God encounters is that once a person meets Him in earnest, there is no denying something happened, something changed. I believe it is impossible to have a true encounter with the Lord and remain the same. His presence in our lives inherently transforms us.

I was taking on a lot of new responsibilities in a foreign academic culture and an educational environment that was not always welcoming to me. My new classmates were interesting. They came from more affluent families with professional backgrounds and clearly had more access to economic and educational privileges. Today, I would describe their mindset as coming from those who are 'entitled' and who expect things to go their way. Back then, I could see and feel the advantages they had, but I was not going to turn around because I had my encounter with God and that moment had assured me that I was moving in the right direction.

When I was most vulnerable, God placed two unlikely teachers in my life to affirm my gifts and encourage me along the way. Although I felt, and sometimes was treated, like a misfit, I was supposed to be there. I knew it. Maybe they knew it too, but did not know how to handle our differences. I was blazing the trail, regardless of their opinions about me. My teachers invited me to have a seat at their proverbial table and I was not willing to give up my seat for anyone.

From my seventh-grade year – excluding math, the bane of my academic life – I was a honor roll student and co-valedictorian in college. When my work ethic, performance, and test scores reflected high academic potential, getting an advanced education became a real option for my future. I believed I was going places, even if I did not have a roadmap, role model, or financial means. I believed God would illuminate the right doors for me to walk through if I continued to be responsible as a student. During my sixth-grade through seventh-grade school years, about the time a young Jewish girl has a bat mitzvah, I put away my childish things and took my passageway to the rest of my future.

CHAPTER 6

PASSAGE OF IDENTITY

"Do not go where the path may lead, go instead where there is no path and leave [blaze] a trail."

Ralph Waldo Emerson

None of us are meant to be duplicates. All of us are one-of-a-kind creations. Identity is to know oneself in a core way that cannot be shaken by happenstance. To know our strengths and weaknesses, to understand our purpose and embrace it, to pursue success and experience failures, to have passions and overcome adversity – all of these experiences help us understand who we are and where we belong. Our children are fearfully and wonderfully made, regardless of the circumstances of their conception. The creation of life is a natural miracle, but the events surrounding their creation may be another story.

Science confirms billions of different cells have to come together at just the right time and in just the right order to produce a healthy baby. There is biological design and complexity in creating life. One chromosome too many, or one too few, can result in life-altering consequences and even fatalities. It is indeed a miracle to conceive and deliver a newborn child. The wonder of this creation should not be taken for granted, considering the myriad of possibilities that could go awry. Women literally put their lives on the line every time they conceive and go into labor.

Children who push their parents to the brink with their strong personality quirks and stubborn willpower are miracles too. I have one, maybe two, of those sons in my household. Each of my sons is gifted and amazing, and they test my mothering skills in different ways. Both of my sons have the same parents, were raised with the same values, and lived in the same homes, but they are unique individuals. Our firstborn son was a great baby. When Elijah was born, he learned to sleep through the night within six months – we counted that a victory. He enjoyed eating whatever we put on his plate and made a conscious effort to be healthy when he was older. He played a lot of sports, and taking naps remains one of his favorite pastimes. He did not cry or complain much as a young child, even when he did not feel well. He was adventurous, which landed him in some trouble at home a time or two. Overall, he was a pleasant child for us to raise as first-time parents and continues to make us extremely proud.

It was ten years later when I had our second son, Ephraim. I was wiser and had more experience with parenting, or maybe not. Ephraim looked just like his older brother when he was younger, but he acted nothing like Elijah. Dave and I lived sleep-deprived for nearly three years, trying everything to get our son to understand sleep was a necessity and he needed to stay in his own room. We had a firm rule: neither of our sons slept in our bed through the night, so once they outgrew the bassinet, it was off to the crib in their room, which was next door. As Ephraim grew up, we knew we had our hands full. He broke the mold for me. I literally gave thanks, told God it was finished, and shut the shop down! Any parenting technique that had worked on Elijah while growing up, failed with Ephraim. Who was this kid, anyway? He was Mr. High Maintenance in a toddler's body. This was a rough season for a military mom.

Through my parenting experience, we acquired the knowledge that parents of multiple children already knew: no two children are the same. Both of our sons had their own identities, personalities, and beliefs, independent of our shared family values. They had different talents, interests, skills, and dreams. It was necessary for me to adapt as their mother, to perceive as their caretaker, and to allow them the space to develop as God created each of them to be with my parental guidance. As they progressed, I struggled in some parenting areas because I tried to control them while keeping pace with the balancing act of providing what they needed in different seasons of their lives. Being their mother remains the most demanding and most rewarding work because I do it with intentionality.

All of these moments of mothering came full circle for me at our 25th Vow Renewal Gala, the second Ferreira family rite of passage ceremony. I did not know the emotions our anniversary ceremony would evoke in our sons. We'd intended to celebrate our covenant relationship with a small gathering of friends and family but as we prepared, the plans shifted to integrating our sons into the ceremony and expanding the gathering. After all, they have skin in our family game too. They'd traveled around the country with us and Elijah had been along for the ride for at least 20 of our 25 years of marriage. Their presence was a return on the investment we'd made into our family and their participation was meaningful to all of us. So, we asked them for their input on the ceremony and kept their ideas in mind while sharing our plans.

As the ceremony preparations unfolded, all of us were excited to celebrate this milestone as a part of our family journey together. Both of them had a significant role in our vow renewal ceremony. Elijah served as his dad's 'best man.' How many sons get to be the best man for their father as he recommits to their mother these days? Not an easy moment to forget. Initially, Elijah and Ephraim both stood at the altar together with us because we were recommitting our marriage and family to God through our own unique expression of love, covenant, and faith. Together, we shared in a generational moment of honor from sons to parents to grandparents. Our sons delivered an eye-watering tribute to us, followed by our parental blessing spoken over their lives. The blessing was complete when the grandsons, bowing down in deference, presenting a gift to their maternal grandmother to acknowledge her presence, and showing respect for her authority as a matriarch in their lives.

During the ceremony, we took inspiration from our holiday tradition to share a Kwanzaa moment, focused on the principle of Umoja (unity), to signify our dedication to working together as a couple and a family. It was a beautiful celebration in which our sons were contributors, not mere spectators. They felt the joy, displayed tears of love, and shared their thoughts during the renewal ceremony. Neither of our sons are married, but both of them know the pride they felt that day at our renewal ceremony. I believe it created an anticipation for them to celebrate covenant and have ceremonies with their children.

The vow renewal was a mountain-peak experience for our family but at some point, we have to travel down the mountain, because mothering presents hills and valleys. Parenting is never more humbling than in a moment when the child teaches the parent without even knowing it. There are plenty of chances to learn from parenting missteps and my son, Ephraim, believes he had most of the answers figured out at the age of eleven. He is brilliant, but brilliance comes with a price tag. Ephraim prospers at whatever he determines to do, but his academic discipline was a slower bloom.

One day he came home from school, during fourth grade, and boldly proclaimed: "Girls are better than boys at everything." I had no warning before this conversation came up. I had no idea how this thought had originated in his mind. Finally, I asked my son why he would say girls are better than boys. He responded, "The teachers like girls more than boys. They always pick girls over boys."

Surprised at his response, I reflected on the demographics of his school, then wondered…Was there validity in his perception that his teachers are drawn to girls, because most teachers are female and girls are more comfortable or familiar to them? Of course, it's human nature to seek familiarity, but at the heart of his issue, he was describing the lack of male teachers in our educational systems, creating a void for young boys who also need to have tangible role models resembling them in the classroom.

Similar to females in male-dominated professions, young boys could be picking up subliminal messages telling them 'girls are better than boys' in a female-dominated environment. I know my son felt a certain way when he came home expressing his frustrations. I wish I could say that was the only time I heard this sentiment of feeling marginalized at school.

We knew Ephraim was enrolled at a terrific school, and parents had to apply in order for their children to attend. The principal and staff were like no other and I was a supportive parent, participating in activities and conversations with his teachers. They had my utmost respect, so his feelings presented a dilemma to me. For his fifth-grade year, we deliberately asked the school to assign him to a male teacher as an experiment, not because the female teachers were less qualified or inadequate. Our son had wonderful teachers, almost exclusively female but I believe learning is enhanced by synergistic teams with multifaceted perspectives. Exposure to cognitive diversity and unfamiliar experiences can increase pathways to learning and growth in children. Listening to my son's plight, I recognized some intangible factor was missing in his learning and it was important to his developmental process.

We were excited when Ephraim got one of the few male teachers in his school. For the first time in his academic career, school resonated and he began demonstrating untapped potential and motivation, and setting academic goals. He came to life in the classroom and was more enthusiastic about his homework. Was he a straight-A student? No, but his attitude and commitment changed. I saw an internal shift in his drive and desire to go to school and perform at his best based on his learning environment. His mindset about work assignments completely changed. He even bragged about his teacher's ability to "bring down the wrath" in the classroom, instilling order and keeping students on a productive path to learning. To that, I shout, Amen!

Exposure to cognitive diversity and unfamiliar experiences can increase pathways to learning and growth in children.

On several occasions, he shared how much he loved being in this teacher's class. Now, maybe he was just a great teacher, but my son had other great teachers at this school, so I believe another variable was at play. Ephraim saw someone who he believed related to him (another male) and it expanded my son's learning reservoir to receive more at school. I ruminated on the implications of his observations, remembering how I'd felt around his age, being the only student who looked like me. How do we get more male representation in our public school systems, which are growing more diverse throughout the nation? Interestingly, school administrators are oftentimes male, even though they work in a female-dominated environment and are rarely seen in a classroom.

As I considered Ephraim's rationale for girls being better, it led me down the path of various 'girl power' and women empowerment movements worldwide. In a female-dominated school environment, could the heightened sensitivity to gender unintentionally cause boys to perceive themselves as left out, in comparison to girls they perceived as being encouraged to excel? For Ephraim, this experience translated into girls being treated differently based on his perception; therefore, girls were better than boys in his female-dominated school.

American public schools, especially primary schools, are resourced with mostly female teachers in the classroom. Just as I applaud a female who advances in a male-dominated system, and I know how challenging that can be, I applaud male teachers who are making a difference in the lives of our children within our educational systems. The impact of the presence of male teachers on our young sons cannot be overstated, since students experience exponentially more female teacher interaction at school.

Ephraim articulated his frustration with the lack of diversity, even as presented in American history, when he came home exclaiming, "Mom, I've had enough of peanuts!" This comment was his response to another lesson on George Washington Carver. It succinctly captured the sentiments of those children who do not see themselves in the curricula and are stuck in a one-dimensional academic system with students who want to learn more.

Parents, this is where we don our teacher hats and step in as educators, sharing our family traditions and cultural history. The burden of teaching children does not rest solely on school teachers. Parents have a duty to educate their children too. Our family has a library of books, not found in public schools, that exposes our children to differences throughout history and culture around the world. We travel to experience other places that are unlike their normal. All of these situations are designed to be educational experiences that help them become caring adults. I want them to be comfortable with themselves and their uniqueness, and appreciate the differences of others. They should not have to ask permission to be who they are. They should not be excluded, either.

Inclusivity can be seen and felt on multiple levels, not just in terms of cultural background, gender, or socioeconomic status. Children need to see themselves reflected in their learning environments and feel like they connect to adults around them as a part of their extended ecosystem. They need positive examples in their lives and encouragement in their academic endeavors. They need to see paths laid out with options for them to believe in dreams, access opportunities, and develop their full potential. American culture and other societies have not been kind to children of color or people who are different when it comes to inclusivity. Our sons were raised in a multicultural family embracing their parents' differences, but by American standards, they are considered Black boys who will be identified as Black men.

In 2009, when Barack Obama became President of the United States of America, my elder son Elijah was six years old. Our family was stationed at Langley Air Force Base and lived in Yorktown, VA. We settled into a suburban, predominantly White middle-class community. It was his first-grade year and midway through it, he realized that no one else in any of his classes looked like him, not a teacher nor a student, and he brought this to our attention. It was the first but not the last conversation about being set apart.

During one of the nightly newscasts, I observed my son staring intently at the television, which seemed odd to me for two reasons: we're not a big news-watching family, and the television had never captured his attention before. I paused to see what held him captivated. In that moment, I noticed he was looking at President Obama and had developed a connection just based on seeing a like image on television. Elijah's earnest response to seeing President Obama in contrast to the landscape of America's history reminded me of the reason Americans adore an underdog story. After all, the 13 colonies were the underdogs in the Revolutionary War! I thought about hit movies like Rudy, Secretariat, Rocky/Creed, and Remember the Titans...all underdogs facing adversity and overcoming the odds, our favorite kind of tales.

Most of the public education curricula limits the achievements of Blacks in America to abolitionists, a few inventors, and civil rights leaders. In the current environment, even those little facts are being chipped away. Indeed, Black people contributed so much more to American society, and the world, than they receive credit for in the American educational system. I believe this is true of other cultural groups as well. In America, children learn primarily about one historical perspective while the recognition of many other Americans' contributions fall abysmally short in the curricula.

As Elijah looked at the television, I watched the gears in his mind processing how the President of the United States stood juxtaposed to his reality of Black Americans left out of American history, and rarely depicted as national leaders. His facial expression signified the mental effort he was making to reconcile the history with this vision of a dignified, Black man and likely the most powerful man in the world at that time. Instinctively, he perceived President Obama as not like other American presidents and this resonated with him on a different level. I was fascinated to behold a visceral experience he could not fully comprehend or articulate. Innocently, he looked up at me with amazement and stated, "The president has hair like mine."

Children are visual learners, and Elijah went directly to what connected him to President Obama: hair. He was captivated, not just because he saw a man with similar skin color, but a man who had a multicultural background with hair like his, and that made a profound impression on him in the first grade. With no prior knowledge of politics or prompting, he naturally picked up on these distinctions at school and home.

Living in a nation that had only elected White, male presidents created an unspoken standard or vision of what an American President of the United States looked like. I know if I were asked that question in first grade, I would have thought of a White man, because that's all I ever saw in that office. It's interesting how Elijah also knew he was not reflected in the presidents of American history at such a young age. Somehow, the message of exclusivity was already infiltrating his reality. His amazement told me that he already recognized that as a boy of his color, he did not have a seat at that leadership table until he saw President Obama, and that moment wrote another chapter in American history that enlarged my son's capacity to envision himself differently.

Mr. Obama's presidential election symbolized inclusivity to people who had been demoralized, unrepresented, and discounted in societies around the world. It was not just a moment for Black Americans; it was a sign of hope for anyone who dreamed a dream against the odds. It was about the promise for little boys and girls of color who could now see possibilities that had never been felt in this way before.

I cannot imagine the psychological pressure and emotional weight that President and First Lady Obama may have experienced as an embodiment of a hopeful change for generations of cultural communities internationally. Children who are raised with consistent, negative portrayals of their communities in movies, television advertisements, and media have a different image than those who are privileged to see themselves reflected in leadership in all industries and careers. Of all the movies about American presidents, none depicted a president of color before Mr. Obama, because it was not true. Maybe some did not believe it to be feasible in America until hope came alive and it was achieved.

Apartheid ended in South Africa around 1994, a few decades after the American Civil Rights Movement of the 1960s. With the abolition of this systemic racial oppression, South Africans elected Nelson Mandela as president. I recall Americans criticizing South African politics, describing it as 'behind the times' because apartheid continued in the 1980s and 1990s. However, while America advanced in civil equality, we did not elect a Black president until 45 years after the Civil Rights Act of 1964. If South Africa was behind the times with apartheid, how could we describe America's delay in electing any person to the presidency who was different than what we've seen for centuries?

Even in other American professions, it was the same story for Black males. Men of color were not seen as Chairman of the Joint Chiefs of Staff until General Colin Powell assumed the position. There was a time when men of color were not considered quarterback material because it was believed they did not have the mental ability to lead on the field. In more recent history, quarterbacks of color, mostly Black men, transformed the game with their play and leadership on the football field. They raised the bar not just for Black quarterbacks, but for all quarterbacks. Their unique presence and abilities to extend plays and run the football, as well as throw it, created a new dynamic and forced other quarterbacks to evolve. Football had a new dimension and the diverse skill sets of quarterbacks expanded the definition of what a quarterback could do and how they could lead.

Society may place limits, but mothers should not put the vision of our children in a proverbial box or allow any system to tell our sons who they are and what they have the ability to become. Historically, America has not been an inclusive society when it comes to gender, race, or ethnicity concerning access to education, healthcare, and economic opportunity. Only in our most recent history are people of color, not just Black people, starting to see themselves in high-visibility leadership roles after hundreds of years of working in, living in, and building this country. People of color have more to offer and educational systems should have more to teach in American history beyond the story of escaped slaves and civil rights.

I am grateful to see more progress than before but it is not sufficient, and that is one reason parents must be teachers also. I look forward to the day when our educational systems embrace the true value of learning with an intent to be inclusive of American history, representing the achievements and failures of all cultures who made this land a success through trial and error. There are many unrecognized heroes who turned the tide of American battles, created inventions, developed medical procedures, and so much more to the benefit of America. Our children, not just children of color, should share in the joy of acknowledging these heroes who sacrificed for this nation and helped it prosper, because we are all benefactors. Their roles should not be minimized to afterthoughts in American history. My sons' experiences showed me another aspect of this daunting reality.

I could have grabbed popcorn and taken pictures while watching Elijah's 'aha' moment. Surprisingly, I felt something I never knew was in my heart. It was both gratifying and sobering. My son would grow up knowing that Black boys, with hair like his, can be presidents too. This is a dream I never had as a child. I am thankful for his paradigm shift, and mine. There are countless boys of color who came before my son who would not dare to dream such lofty dreams. It was deemed an impossibility, and Black men died without this hope coming to fruition. As a mother, I do not want boundaries placed on my sons' abilities or future potential. No system or authority has the right to steal or block anyone's dreams or visions of achieving if they are willing to earn it.

My mother-son moment was not political. The politics of the day were not my focus, because the sentiment was much deeper. My son was not of voting age; he did not care about the rhetoric. It was a tender moment of observing his realization of the America he was born into and the fact that American history just expanded to include representation of his people in the highest office of the land. He saw a man on television who reflected a version of what he saw in the mirror daily. I was stunned that it all started with hair.

It is easy to treat as common what is familiar, readily available, or frequently experienced. People can take for granted the privilege of subconscious, collective learning, and how powerful it is to see reflections of oneself in the early stages of life. Individuals belonging to underrepresented communities did not have this life advantage, but still they dreamed. They could believe in a day that would be better, where they too were intentionally included and welcomed, and not because the law demanded it but because they were appreciated. Wouldn't it be wonderful for children to think such dreams are attainable, where they are free to offer their talents equitably and be recognized for making positive contributions to their schools, organizations, and communities?

America does not have a shortage of domestic problems to solve. Globally, we are competing with adversarial leaders who are closing the gap. We are unwise to think our American foundation cannot be shaken. It already has been, and the attacks of September 11, 2001, were evidence that we are not impenetrable. Wise leaders would realize we are in no position to gamble with our children's future and devour ourselves by rejecting any American who can and wants to contribute to our collective success as a sovereign nation. We need all Americans, of all backgrounds, volunteering to serve and lead for the sake of future generations.

Our nation cannot withstand being a divided house and the status quo will not hold up in a global economy rapidly and violently transforming around us. I call this refusal to shift from an outdated way of thinking the 'Blockbuster Syndrome.' It is believing what America has to offer is so superior that we do not need to examine ourselves or evolve because we could never be unseated. It appeared to be Blockbuster Video's mentality as it watched Redbox, Netflix, Amazon, and a host of other competitors change the game. Blockbuster went from being a staple of entertainment to now, not even being mentioned. By the time they realized they could be replaced, evidently, it was too late to recover. Pride comes before the fall. Presumably, there was no leadership foresight or cognitive diversity to bring a different perspective about the importance of evolving with the digital age percolating at its doorstep. It was a strategic oversight that led to its downfall.

As a nation, America is on the verge of change. It is at our doorstep and change is not asking our permission. We do not have the power to hold back change. There is a reason for extinction and failed nations. Usually, it involves pride, strife, and the inability to adapt and overcome adversity together. I hung up a picture of one of President Obama's speeches in my sons' play area, something I did not intend to do until I witnessed the positive response it evoked in Elijah. I wanted a tangible reminder for him to recall what he saw and how he felt at that moment. I knew the climate would change over his lifetime, but I hoped he could look at that picture and see a symbol of encouragement for his leadership journey when times got hard. I wanted Elijah and Ephraim to think beyond the limitations that others may try to place on them. Most importantly, I needed them to internalize an image of greatness within them because they were created for much more. Ultimately, identity is found in knowing who they are in Christ first, and visible role models can be powerful reminders.

As a mother of Black sons, I know the world can be harsh, unkind, and unforgiving to them. It pains me to admit it but all is not equal, not yet. History is replete with stories of black and brown people losing their lives over senseless acts of violence, abuse of authority, and the inability to relate to others to de-escalate conflict. The power of exposure and access to education and learning opportunities is a portal. My sons, like yours, must believe they belong in American society as equals, not subordinates. The desire for equality and equity are inherent in humanity but neglected all too often for children of color who get left behind.

In the early years of Elijah's life, America was the most powerful country, and elected an African American as president. Before that time, it was rare for Black Americans to see what Elijah saw growing up with as his normal depiction of an American president and it happened during a critical stage of his social development. He would never have to wonder what it would be like to have a president who looked like him. How differently his self-perception, and that of other Black people in general, was being shaped in contrast to the Black communities of the 1950s, 1960s, and previous generations.

American political agendas and monolithic narratives about groups of people are disguises that hinder our ability to see the real enemy operating in our nation. Without vision, there is no unity of purpose or real progression, creativity is diminished, and children suffer because they are extraordinary dreamers. Their ideas and concepts are seeds and the imagination is the creative space for them to develop and mature. Before anything can manifest in our natural world, it must first originate as a thought in the imagination. Vision proceeds manifestation, so there is no reason to limit a child's ability to dream of a better life for themselves and others. If America continues on divisive pathways, there is a buffet of societal ills waiting for an opportune time to ensnare our sons.

Isolation and rejection breed insecurity in young men, causing them to question their identity and even resort to less honorable ways to prove their worth. Sharing my experiences about the first African-American President of the United States and the oversaturation of female educators in the classroom may cause some consternation and some 'spidey senses' to begin to tingle, but remember this discourse is about raising our sons to discover their identities and become leaders, at home and in a diverse society. Their self-perceptions are influenced at early ages by those they see and interact with on a regular basis. It is a fact that America elected an African-American president for two terms. In 2021, female teachers outnumbered male teachers in America's public education systems three to one, on average. Data sources show an average of 75-80 percent of public school teachers in the United States are female, specifically White females.[iv]

> *Before anything can manifest in our natural world, it must first originate as a thought in the imagination.*

Let me pause to commend all educators who accept the challenge of teaching our youth. You are amazing! Teachers in America are not valued enough and certainly not paid according to their worth, but that is another conversation. My point is that the demographics and lack of consideration for America's diverse history leave room for improvement in our educational system nationwide. Every school should promote cognitive diversity to increase their students' exposure to learning something new.

There are unintended consequences in a profession that does not attract and retain a diverse workforce and education is not excluded. Teachers, like other professions, need the ability to relate to all types of people from various backgrounds and life experiences in a way that makes learning equitable for all students. Familiarity is a part of learning and there can be an academic disconnect in the classroom environment if students feel neglected, misunderstood, or as if they do not belong. Statistically, American schools are dominated by one demographic of teachers who are stepping up to answer the call. Let me say it again: I applaud all the teachers in the classroom because they are showing up every day for our children. As a mom who volunteered at my sons' schools, I am impressed by the excellent teachers I have encountered, many of whom are now exiting the school system due to persistent, systematic barriers that are killing their passion to teach.

Teachers deserve our appreciation and better compensation as key members of our children's community. The COVID-19 pandemic was validation that I am not meant to be a school teacher. I pray for those brave souls who are in the trenches daily. It is a tough and at times undervalued job and not every teacher can perform well, so this leaves children unsupported in some areas pertaining to their self-worth, potential, and identity. Some may say it is the parents' job to cultivate their children's identity and worth, and I wholeheartedly agree; however, most children spend more hours with teachers than parents. The reality is that we need a strategic partnership between home, schools, and community to produce the best outcomes for children. In a learning environment, teachers must cultivate belonging, appreciation for differences, and understanding of other perspectives. This is a formidable task when teachers are hindered by governing leadership and uninspiring curricula.

Life lessons and experiences are also good teachers. The need for social connection to others who can relate to our personal experience produces empathy and this is critical in academic environments. I learned first-hand that it is difficult for students of color to excel in academic environments when they are not accepted. It is harder for employees to advance in professional workplaces when they are not welcomed based on their race, ethnicity, religion, or gender. Until this attitude of exclusivity changes, an unfair burden rests on underrepresented and underserved children and they have to learn to navigate and push through it to succeed in academia, corporations, and established systems in public and private industry.

The nation we build today comes with lingering effects for our children and grandchildren tomorrow. It will not improve if we do not improve in our productive conversations, and stay rooted in truth and facts, not political rhetoric or personal comfort. I am addressing sensitive subjects, but a responsible society prioritizes intelligent and compassionate discourse. It does not ignore truth and cling to familiarity. It does not allow unmerited fear to govern reasonable discussions that could move us toward growth and solidarity. The reason we must address this discomfort is that without dealing with it, as parents, we cannot fortify our sons and daughters to handle their own discomforts in what appears to be a volatile, uncertain, complex, and ambiguous world.

> *The nation we build today comes with lingering effects for our children and grandchildren tomorrow.*

As parents, there are things we do not fully understand and cannot explain. However, there are other things we do understand and we should explain to our children. When left unaddressed, parents pass along the same generational and societal dysfunctions that do not build resiliency in our children or increase their respect for others and life in general.

Every person's life should matter to other human beings. Regardless of their background, children will experience some form of pain and suffering. They will have disappointments and rejection. Will we, as parents and collective guardians, equip them with the resources to overcome the inevitable trials of life? I hope your answer is a resounding "Yes, we will," because I am talking about building leaders of leaders.

Leaders cannot hide behind walls of ease and seek popularity. Being a leader of principle and conviction is not for the faint of heart. We must groom sons who are comfortable enough with discomfort to walk in personal integrity, with courage, even when they have to walk alone. To maneuver in this space, they must be secure in their own identities, and it is up to parents to help our sons foster a stronger sense of self-worth and empathy as they grow into leaders.

Rites of Passage

CHAPTER 7
PASSAGE OF CHARACTER AND INTEGRITY

"The lesser of two evils is still evil."

Lessons in Chemistry

I was born on Patuxent River Naval Air Station, located in St. Mary's County, Maryland, as a dependent of Jesse L. Hansley, Sr. He retired as a Navy Boatswain Mate and he was the only dad I've ever known. He was my maternal grandfather and I affectionately called him 'Grandpop,' even though he was more of a father to me. I grew up in a household where ten children had passed through before my arrival. We were by no stretch of the imagination middle class but I did not go hungry, unless by choice. I was comforted knowing I belonged to my family and was accountable to a community. I felt safe there.

I grew up recognizing the families in my neighborhood and they knew me and my family. Grandpop grew wonderful fruit trees, gardens of flowers and vegetables, real food, and I was the carrier of different garden products to our neighbors at my grandmother's bidding.

We also received some fresh produce from others in the community, like kale from Mr. Norman's garden, and he wasn't even in our neighborhood.

In this life you have two things - your word and your name. Take good care of them because once you lose them, they are hard to get back.

- Jesse L. Hansley, Sr.

From my perspective, we did not waste anything, including food, water, and electricity. I thought it was because we were good stewards. I did not consider myself underprivileged or lacking any necessities. My family consistently opened our home to others and the kitchen was in business with home-cooked meals daily to share with those in need; we even invited individuals to live with us if they did not have refuge. We seemed to adopt people and continually grow our family. My grandparents' house was a home, a family gathering place, and people could drop in and find hospitality. I saw true compassion, leadership, and service in action. We did not just talk about values, we lived them.

It was not until I went to middle school that I felt out of place, like I was not on par with my peers because I came from a different socioeconomic and racial background than all of my classmates. They taught me that I was different, excluded me, and treated me with little regard until my breakout years in high school. By then, I'd learned to embrace the family values ingrained in me and most of my core identity was firmly established; living by standards and knowing my identity were assets that propelled me into being a better person and leader.

The lifestyle my grandparents afforded me as a child became my foundation for living. It is why I discern the importance of caring for people around me at home, in the marketplace, and in my community. I live in a 'middle-class' neighborhood and I don't grow gardens – in fact, I don't like digging in the dirt at all – but I practice charity and kindness. When I buy too much fresh produce, I share it with my neighbor. For no particular reason, I'll make fresh tea from leaves and roots or homemade dessert and drop it off for them to enjoy too.

Growing up in my childhood community was where I initially learned that character and integrity matter, service on behalf of others is good, and if I wasn't going to do something right the first time, then "don't do it at all." The Air Force core values of Integrity First, Service Before Self, and Excellence in All You Do were second nature to me, because that was all I knew while growing up with parents who demonstrated those principles. My Grandpop is in heavenly rest but his essence is alive and well in me and his great grandchildren. My sons are recipients of my parents' teachings about love, hard work, cleanliness, and discipline that they cultivated in me and I practice similar standards in raising my children.

Ironically, I do not recall a single conversation with my grandfather about values and principles beyond the one statement of keeping my word and a good name. He was a man of few words and great action. I simply paid attention to the consistency in his life. It took being an officer in the Air Force to genuinely tap into his essence as a leader and his absence when he passed. My life was shaped by my family and a community upbringing in which I inherited cultural traditions. It was not evident to me as a child but, as I reflect, I know now that those values, principles, and traditions are inextricably integrated into my being.

There are lessons my Grandpop taught me, and none more life-changing than my favorite quote from him: "In this life you have two things – your word and your name. Take good care of them because if you lose them, they are hard to get back." I listened to his wisdom on maintaining character and integrity as a 21-year-old woman, standing on his front porch while preparing to cross the country with my new husband. His sage advice may not seem earth-shattering at first, but try practicing it daily in everything you do. It's a choice I make every day, every moment. Try keeping your word and reputation above reproach to the point that when you speak, people do not question whether it is coming from a noble intent. Let the goodness of your character proceed your presence, creating a desire for people to want you around personally and professionally because you bring care and honor with you.

Nothing builds trust and self-confidence like an honorable reputation. Nothing brings peace of mind like living a life of integrity. Truly, nothing brings

Jesse L. Hansley, Sr. being sworn in for reenlistment

adversity more than standing as a person of character and principle.

I can stand on my words and actions, even when I make a mistake, because my integrity covers faults. Actually, integrity keeps me from making more mistakes. When a person is known to be honest and authentic, they do not have to fear being ousted or discovered to be something they are not. They live with integrity as a foundation for their words and their actions align with their life decisions. The trait I loved most about my Grandpop was that he was a man of his word – 100 percent. If he said it, he meant it. He did not speak a lot but when he spoke, it carried significant weight. He epitomized Matthew 5:37; just a simple "Yes, I will" or "No, I won't" is all that is required. When he said "Yes," I could take it to the bank without worrying about insufficient funds to back it up.

Living a life of integrity matters, even when God is the only One who can see what you did or hear the very thought in your heart. It ALL matters.

This same lesson is what I set out to teach my sons – character matters. Living a life of integrity matters, even when God is the only One who can see what you did or hear the very thought in your heart. It ALL matters. The reason I've reiterated these words to my sons throughout their lives is because I want them to internalize this principle so they have the power to guard their words and actions. Character will stand up to help them avoid questionable behaviors, and integrity will protect them against shady business ethics so they pursue higher ideals. The person who said "ignorance is bliss" had a keen perspective. Sometimes, the weight of walking in integrity is heavy and hard to bear. Some days, I just don't want to know the reality of what I know. It is a blessing and a responsibility to be a person of good character and to live a life of integrity, particularly in environments that do not advocate those virtues.

In parts of the world, honor is a relic. It hurts to hear children speak to their parents as if there was some spiritual authority granted to children to command their parents on how they should be raised. I am appalled by the parents who allow disrespectful behaviors in the name of love or friendship with their children. Mothers, hear me, please. While we are raising our children, we are not meant to be their primary friends. We are parents with a charge to raise upstanding children who can lead in their families and communities, maybe even nations, with character and integrity. We cannot allow our personal desire to be besties in our children's eyes to be a motivator in how we parent and prepare them for adult life. I am convinced that if my sons love everything I do as a mother, there's something I'm not doing right. I love my sons enough to discipline them so they learn right from wrong, and it does not feel good to me or them. Yet, it is precisely this type of training that will teach them to have regard for themselves and other people, and to temper their words and behaviors. Are these not the type of leaders we want in our society – leaders who care about integrity and other people?

My sons will never be equal to me in spiritual authority, but they are still valuable and important people. Their place in my life as sons comes with a lifelong obligation to show deference, honor, and respect to me and any elder, always! They cannot outgrow their position. No matter what, they will always be my sons. My grandchildren will not be equal to my sons, because that is not the order established in the family. In Ephesians chapter 6, God commands: "Children, obey your parents because you belong to the Lord, for this is the right thing to do. Honor your father and mother. This is the first commandment with a promise: If you honor your father and mother, things will go well for you, and you will have a long life on the earth." I want my sons to live righteously and have a long, healthy life on the earth. God gives this promise to children, but it comes with conditions – obedience and honor.

Due to our storied past, it can be offensive to say my sons are 'not equal' to me, because of the emotional triggers associated with the shameful history of American slavery and the denial of civil liberties for women and people of color. These generational wounds can make the truth hard to face and even more difficult for some to discuss. It is compounded by leadership hypocrisy and abuse of authority on local, state, national, and international stages.

When I refer to my sons as not being equal to me, that means my role and position in their lives is that of a teacher or guide, not the other way around. Children should not raise their parents. Certainly, I can learn from them, but their position is not that of a teacher to me. I am not referring to inequality as it pertains to their humanity or rights as human beings to live with the same dignity everyone deserves. I am speaking to the need to have structure and healthy respect for proper authority figures to shape values and check wrong attitudes or misconduct. There is no place for abusive authority of any kind from anyone. Oppression and suppression, of any group of people, is ungodly and immoral behavior, no matter where it resides. We should never condone or be complicit in abuse of any kind. It takes character and integrity to insist on everyone being treated with dignity and respect.

Genesis chapters 1-2 provide the account of God delegating authority over the earth. When sin entered the world, so did immorality, including greed, violence, and evil desires to oppress people for personal gain. Later, in Ephesians 5, God explains the order for marriage by designating the husband as the leader of his family, not its oppressor. In God's Kingdom, the leader is the greatest servant so, with proper understanding of authority, husbands should be the first to serve in their homes. Likewise, this leadership principle applies across spectrums. Leaders serve rather than dominate people. Domination and control do not equate to leadership.

In America, we are consumed by personal rights to the point of our rights colliding with our morals. Some people have an exaggerated sense of entitlement. They think it is their right to have and do what they please, when they please. This type of egocentric thinking does not mix well with a civil or peaceful society and we are seeing the fallout that comes from this self-serving mentality. We have civil war brewing over morality, rights, and principles of equality and equity.

When leadership is mixed with compassion and integrity, we can increase peace in our homes, schools, workplaces, and communities. If we raise sons who believe in serving, we will produce leaders who believe in serving others personally and professionally. If we raise sons who are entitled, they will lead from a place of entitlement and pride, lacking in moral character to serve anyone beyond their own selfish ambitions. Have we not seen this type of prideful leadership unleashed in various places, from governments and workplaces, to religious institutions, and even in families?

Selfishness defiles the culture of any environment and destroys the sense of belonging in that community. An attitude of entitlement and pride breeds corrupt hearts and leaders focused on self-interest and self-promotion, not the goodwill of those they are called to serve.

Mothers have a critical role in raising our sons to come up to the standard of moral leadership. Why do I focus on mothers? Because women are usually carriers of compassion. Of course, men can be compassionate too, but men do not have a maternal instinct to nurture. The type of husbands our sons learn to become is correlated to interpersonal dynamics learned from their mothers too. It is important for mothers to teach how they expect their sons to act as leaders, husbands, and fathers. Training our sons to be honorable men is a lot of work and it takes sacrifice, but what is the alternative? There is no other way to instill character and integrity without training and guidance from mothers and fathers.

Babies are so wonderful...and exhausting! They do not have compassion for their parents or exercise restraint. They do not stop to consider if their constant need to eat is disrupting their mother's sleep. Mothers know how selfish (and cute) their precious newborn babies are, and most people cuddle them. Ask those same people to babysit a newborn and watch their reaction. Those who have matriculated past the newborn cuteness season usually wait to babysit until children are fully potty-trained and sleeping through the night. While these demanding behaviors are tolerable in newborn babies, they are not sustainable or acceptable as our sons grow up. We get trapped by thinking that age will cause children to change on their own, and that may happen in some cases, but not when it comes to character and integrity.

Integrity is not a part-time job. It requires devotion to principle and self-assessment on a daily basis.

These values must be cultivated because human beings are born selfish, and without proper training, they will remain selfish. A selfish nature is innate in all of us and it does not just dissipate over time; it requires correction to develop at each phase of life. If our young sons are not taught to be caring, they will grow into uncaring older sons. It is an arduous process to instill children with integrity and character. It requires an enormous amount of persistence and consistency. My younger son is still in the process of learning to be more forthright with his intentions at times. I remind him that honesty is the standard, even if there are negative consequences. Children may not see the benefit of living with integrity and that is the reason parents have to insist on it.

Back to my Grandpop's words of wisdom. I see them as a verbal rite of passage for me. I did not know it at the time, but his words were the foundation and culmination of my personal life and professional career concisely summed up in three words: walk in integrity. Integrity is not a part-time job. It requires devotion to principle and self-assessment on a daily basis. It even insists on humility and acknowledging when I am wrong. Sometimes I am not at fault, but I apologize to make relationships right again, because people are more important to me than ego. When our sons see this level of humility and vulnerability, they also learn they can be humble instead of prideful. They can be transparent instead of secretive.

During my time in the military and other leadership roles, I mentored young, transitioning adults. At every opportune moment, I passed on my dad's wisdom that he'd shared with me. It never failed to strike a chord with someone who needed to hear it.

We live in a society that tells our sons that the ends justify the means, but this is not always true. I do not want my sons thinking they can get ahead by any means necessary. Reflecting on this cliché caused me to consider the number of phrases we repeat without evaluating them for moral accuracy. Human reasoning, apart from moral standards, usually brings dishonor to others.

Jesus demonstrated how to overcome the temptation of relying only on human wisdom to accomplish our objectives. In Matthew chapter 4, Jesus is led into the wilderness for a time of testing, which lasted forty days. One temptation was to test his character or pride by suggesting He throw Himself off a pinnacle in order to prove who Jesus already knew He was, the Son of God. Satan tried to entice Jesus into taking an action, other than God's will to sacrifice His life on a cross, to provide redemption for the world. Satan offered Jesus the 'by any means necessary' approach. If Jesus yielded to the temptation of pride, He would have tried to do God's will in the world's way.

The world looks for spectacular displays; God uses a righteous life. Jesus knew He was sent to redeem people from sin and that is what mattered. In knowing His identity and purpose, He understood redemption had to take place by His death on a cross, not by throwing Himself off a pinnacle to prove a senseless point. He could have negated His entire purpose by falling into pride and ego, but He was not deceived by this trick to test His character and we should not be deceived either.

> *The world looks for spectacular displays; God uses a righteous life.*

God's way of seeing the world and relating to our situations comes through a much broader lens and more compassionate view than most can understand. He was there in our past, is with us in the present, and sees our future. His way is not limited or predicated on our human reasoning. He knows the world He created and observes it from a different vantage point so He can guide us in making the right decisions. Individuals, and consequently societies, are enticed to think our way is the only or right way. We compromise ethics and fight with any and everyone around us to get our way. By keeping our own counsel, we are only doing what is right in our own eyes and we, inevitably, get off-course.

Our children can be led astray in their way of thinking and behaving by the example their parents set before them. Parents cannot teach humility if they are prideful, and pride leads to destructive paths. We make a grave mistake if we do not take time to listen to our sons' concerns and allow them to make some choices and mistakes that develop their character. The key here is to realize that all mistakes are not equal.

We have to guide our sons in a way that allow mistakes that lead to growth and avoid mistakes that pull them away from their purpose. There is a time for mothers to exercise restraint and permit consequences, as they have valuable lessons. There is also a time to stand and fight against destructive powers trying to take our children down. Life would be much easier if we did not have to make tough decisions or experience hurt, but what kind of life would that be? We must face temptations, live with imperfect people, and make difficult decisions because we are not robots.

God gets a lot of blame for things that people do not understand when situations go awry in the world. Sin and all of its derivatives corrupted a perfect world, so there is no escape from hardship or absence of suffering in this life for anyone. We all are negatively impacted by the evil that exists and it is not fair when children die, spouses get sick, or life takes a bad turn for 'good' people. God did not cause this pain in the world. It is the nature of sin and evil desires that produces suffering. The good news is that God will help us face and overcome these difficulties, and we have to do our part in aligning our decisions with His plans.

Remember our discourse on the main thing – we all choose to worship something: careers, pride, religious piety, human intellect, earthly possessions, or God. It is all a choice and there is no middle ground in idolatry. Everyone will serve something or someone, and each parent makes the choice and teaches their children what to value by default.

Integrity and character must be passed on to every generation for any society to be moral. Producing men with character and integrity may run countercultural, because society may legalize or permit behaviors that are inconsistent with the character traits that some mothers want to develop in their sons. These cultural shifts do not negate the parental call to uphold the standard. After all, society did not give birth to our sons; mothers did.

CHAPTER 8

PASSAGE OF SUFFERING WITH GRATITUDE

"It will never get easier...
you handle hard better."

Kara Lawson

The Queen of Complaining – that was me. If I did not like it, you knew about it. It was written all over my face and I had no issue telling people, directly I might add, what I thought the problem was and how to get it straight. My motives were well-intended, and I was not malicious – but my approach just sucked! With maturity and conviction from the Holy Spirit, I learned that not all truths need to be spoken and, when they are, the timing matters and the message should be flavored with compassion.

In the past, my words were not seasoned with grace or gratitude. Since I struggled to curtail reckless words, I had to receive spiritual discipline, and that was one of the best things for my personal development because it resulted in my growth as a leader. Over the course of three intense days, I got an attitude adjustment from pride. It changed my attitude and behaviors, which changed the course of my life. To win in life is never easy, we learn and grow through adversity.

Mothers normally want obedient and reverent children, but some also want to forgo the training process with the discipline required to produce those qualities. It is natural to want to avoid pain and alleviate suffering, especially for our children. Mothers make great sacrifices to circumnavigate unpleasant conditions for our children but, inevitably, they must go through difficulties sometimes because there can be purpose in the pain. I do not believe God sends suffering, but He may allow us to experience suffering that comes from living in a world where people operate with evil intentions. It is a consequence, and even Jesus was not spared pain and suffering.

To win in life is never easy, we learn and grow through adversity.

As parents, we can underestimate these moments of suffering our children must go through to mature and learn obedience. Hebrews 5:7-8 is an interesting scripture because it states that when Jesus was on the earth, He offered prayers and pleadings, with a loud cry and tears, to the One who could rescue Him from death. Even though Jesus was God's Son, He also learned obedience from the things He suffered. I cannot comprehend the particulars of how or when God chose to answer Jesus' prayers but I know, regardless of the answer, Jesus suffered to the point of death. He took the suffering I deserved, in my disobedience and sin towards God, so I could learn to walk in obedience to God. As a mother, I am convicted by those verses. How can I desire to alleviate all suffering for my sons and expect them to learn obedience if my Savior had to suffer, if I had to suffer? I did not learn obedience without going through some pain in life, and neither did you. Everyone will suffer something at some time. When suffering is absent, obedience may be delayed because learning from consequences is a prerequisite for maturity. Children may continue to 'take another lap' in their development if parents do not allow them to mature through the passage of suffering.

Unfortunately, as a mother, I reproduced after my own kind and passed on the undesirable trait of complaining. My youngest son is incredibly perceptive and articulate, but lacks restraint with words. When he feels a certain way, he believes he is entitled to say it, regardless of the time or place. As I listened to my son's complaints, I realized he had good points, but his approach did not motivate me to listen to the message.

Entitlement is a belief that the world is one big Burger King, who famously coined the phrase 'have it your way.' Some mothers contribute to their sons' belief in a 'have-it-your-way' world: a place where they are entitled to what they want, when they want, and how they want it, without the understanding of there being 'a time and place' for all things. Entitlement is a virus of this generation, and mothers are a cure to keep our sons from being infected. The have-it-your-way mentality applies to hamburgers, not raising men of standard.

115

When children believe they are superior to others, above the rules, or entitled to what they want regardless of the consequences, they are in harm's way. They also put others in harm's way. We should not allow suffering unnecessarily, but there is a reason that children need to pass through suffering if our sons are to grow into men and leaders.

In the original Marvel movie, *Thor*, his father, King Odin, demonstrates a most effective lesson on training and discipline between a father and son, or a king and soon-to-be king. Although King Odin is angry with Thor's behaviors, leading their realm to the "horrors of war and death," he tries to teach Thor the errors of his childish, impulsive, and short-sighted perspective. When Thor refuses to be counseled by his father and disrespects him in front of his younger brother, Odin switches roles from father to king. Although he has parental authority, he speaks to his son as a ruler by stripping Thor of his position, title, and all the power the king has entrusted to him as the Prince of Asgard.

Before King Odin takes this drastic measure, he tries to talk with his son. Odin warns Thor that his words are "pride and vanity talking, not leadership." Thor retorts with an insult to his father that pushes King Odin to make an example of his son. Odin, no longer speaking as a father, replies in utter disappointment to Thor's rebelliousness: "You are a vain, greedy, cruel boy." Ashamed of his son's stubbornness displayed in this moment, Odin admits that "I was a fool to think you were ready" to be king. It is a convicting statement about his feelings of failure as a father and leader.

Finally, the king silences Thor by declaring, "You are unworthy of these realms, you are unworthy of your title, and unworthy of the loved ones you betrayed." Then, he pronounces his judgment: "I now take from you your Power, in the name of my father and his father before, I Odin Allfather, cast you out." With this pronouncement, King Odin physically strips Thor of all relics and power inherited through his name and title then throws Thor down to earth, but the scene does not end there.

As Thor is falling from the heavens, King Odin picks up Thor's weapon, a mighty hammer, and whispers, "Whoever holds the hammer, if he is worthy, shall possess the power of Thor." This final statement reveals the king's true intent to raise his son into a man of integrity and character, one who is worthy of being a future king. Even in his anger, caused by Thor's disobedience and dishonor which forced Odin to discipline his out-of-control son, the king keeps hoping that Thor will one day become worthy again. It is a powerful parenting moment, because King Odin understands that if Thor is ever going to be the leader of Asgard, he cannot downplay Thor's character flaws. Thor must grow up.

When Thor could no longer heed the teachings of his father, suffering the loss of all his privileges, discipline was necessary to reset the boundaries and produce the character of a king. Spoiler alert: Thor gets the revelation, but not before he has to suffer some pain and humiliation. In reaching the end of his childish self, he becomes a man who is ready to lead. All of our sons need some form of Thor's lesson. At the end, father and son are speaking in private about their journey:

Odin: *"You'll be a wise king"*

Thor: *"There will never be a wiser king or a better father. I have much to learn and I know that now."[vii]*

This scene depicts the intent of parental authority and proper use of discipline when enforcing consequences to train future leaders. I've never cast my sons down from heaven, but I have exerted my authority to get them back into proper alignment. It never felt good to do so but I knew it was necessary for their good.

In 2022, I watched a series called *Limitless* with Chris Hemsworth, the actor who plays Thor. I wasn't sure what to expect but once I watched the first episode, my view shifted. The goal of the series was to promote health, longevity, and acceptance of life in community. He was put through some extreme but meaningful tasks with the intent of teaching him appreciation for his life and the people who supported him. To learn those lessons, he suffered and gained the opportunity to become a greater husband, father, brother, and son. I vicariously reaped a small benefit from the show, because it increased my appreciation for the gift of family. Thank you, Mr. Hemsworth!

We have moments that remind us of our humanity and how no one, not even our fictional heroes, is exempt from suffering. The beauty Mr. Hemsworth found in this universal experience of pain is balanced with his maturity. The transformation he undergoes through his adventures exemplify the reason parents cannot afford to raise entitled children who are unable to see beyond their desires or withstand the trials they will inevitably face in life. An easy life may not produce a good leader. Somehow, in our development, particularly in modern cultures filled with conveniences, the 'good life' equates to being devoid of struggle, hard work, and suffering, so we think. Parents learn to associate suffering with negativity and discount the virtue it could hold with the positive effects of growth and obedience in the process. I don't know a parent who does not want their children to listen and obey instructions. I have never heard a parent say, "I wish my kids would stop listening to me and do whatever they want to do," have you? If I could patent obedience and sell it, I wouldn't be able to manufacture it fast enough for parents. Maybe suffering has been underestimated as an ingredient to develop endurance, patience, humility, strength, and resilience because not all suffering is evil.

I do not believe there is substantial development or personal growth without the passage of suffering. It is natural to want an easier path laden with conveniences. However, emotional underdevelopment is costly and it limits the ability to handle the complexities of a world filled with hurt people, broken relationships, financial challenges, and personal disappointments. We must enable our sons' potential to blossom and connect to others in a considerate, more understanding way if they are to lead effectively. Who understands the loss of a child, catastrophe of divorce, or battle with illness more than the people who journey through and overcome it? Some may say they are stronger because of it. Experience is an excellent teacher if we are willing to grow through the pain. The ability to support, coach, and mentor our children flows out of various seasons in life. These moments offer an entrance to another level of maturity.

Gratitude is an underrated weapon against suffering. A grateful person is not consistently overcome by negativity, fear, depression, or loss because gratitude bolsters mental and emotional resilience. It reminds us of the reasons to keep moving forward and it is why I emphasize practicing the skill of sincerely saying "thank you" with my sons. Gratitude is a mindset, a choice we make daily. It is nearly impossible to have heartfelt gratitude and remain down in the dumps. Something about remembering the good, in the midst of the bad, changes us from the inside out.

Emotionally underdeveloped adults are everywhere, and it is a perilous sight to see the unhealed trauma all around. Hurting adults receive the same legal rights as other adults, but they lack the emotional maturity to use them wisely, so we see bad decisions and worse consequences inflicted on society. Rejection, trauma, grief, or personal struggles can leave some people unequipped to transition safely into adulthood. Through moments of suffering properly, children can develop a balanced perspective, stability, and resilience in the face of difficulties. One 'beautiful gift' our sons have obtained through suffering is the ability to express empathy. Without suffering, they would not have compassion. Without compassion, they cannot develop proper perspective as leaders.

Revelation chapter 12 paints a vivid picture of a great battle with an eternally evil adversary set on destruction. It is specific in noting the enmity against mothers and their children, but we defeat our enemy by having faith in Jesus and His redemptive work on the cross, and holding fast to our personal testimony. Ironically, a testimony only comes after passing through a test. Adversity is meant to strengthen our capabilities and allow our sons to discover what they could not obtain apart from trials and testing. No matter who we are, where we come from, or our economic status in life, we cannot be free of consequences in a world where evil resides. Evil cannot be eradicated from this world but it can be overcome with good.

In Genesis 4:7, God is having a conversation with Cain before Cain murders his brother, Abel. God forewarns Cain by declaring, "You will be accepted if you do what is right. But if you refuse to do what is right, then watch out! Sin (evil) is crouching at the door, eager to control you. But you must subdue it and be its master." We all have opportunities to refine our character by examining our thoughts, attitudes, and words to ensure they align with moral behaviors. In his book, *Experiencing God Devotional*, Henry Blackaby illustrates the correlation between preparation in life, decision-making, and suffering, stating, "Temptations come at unexpected moments. At the moment of conviction, you must master the sin that crouches at the door of your life… you will avoid unnecessary hardship for yourself and others."[viii] When parents prepare their children for the time of adversity, they are positioning them to overcome evil and hardships.

If a child's behaviors do not conform to expectations, this is called 'acting out' of character. Literally, it means the child's outward actions are not demonstrating the inward principles taught and they are behaving outside of the set boundaries, usually showing disrespect or lack of self-control. Freedom is a wonderful privilege that comes at a great price. Any freedom, without restraint, creates an overindulgent appetite and makes an overindulgent society a prisoner of its own greed and selfishness. Just like with children, too much freedom comes with a side effect of societal 'acting out' of set boundaries and sometimes trespassing against other peoples' boundaries. Wrong attitudes towards displeasures or adversity lead to wrong behaviors and, at times, tragic and unnecessary suffering.

Suffering can be a scalpel that cuts away unkind edges and increases our capacity to live with others in humility. During the passage of suffering, our sons will be matured and become resilient enough to stand against the temptations that will come to entrap them. Suffering is a rite and everyone must drink from the cup. It is futile to try to alleviate all pain for our children. Even if that were possible, by doing so, we are likely to present to society a person we did not intend. We should endeavor to teach our children to lean into their moments of suffering by equipping them with resources to leverage their painful experiences for their good and the benefit of others.

I know suffering is not enjoyable, and I don't like it either, but that does not mean it has no purpose or value. The passage of suffering would be demoralizing if there were no upside, but that is where gratitude steps in. Gratitude is a proven and effective weapon against the negative effects of suffering. Negative reactions, fear, and sadness are normal responses to some situations, but individuals are not meant to live in a constant state of anxiety and distress. I am not dismissing medical reasons for these conditions, but I believe gratitude can bolster one's defenses against them.

Being thankful is a mechanism planted in each of us and we choose to activate it, or not, when life attacks our will and mind. When situations are weighing me down, I look to the things that renew my thoughts and bring fresh perspectives to what I am going through. This form of gratefulness helps temper my temptation to complain and be negative. Gratitude functions like a guardrail in my heart, providing protection and recalibrating my thoughts to align with truth and not just the facts of my current dilemma. Gratitude may not change the circumstances we face, but it can change us inwardly.

You should be generous with gratitude. It does not cost a thing but it is priceless.

In the Harvard Health Publishing article, "Giving Thanks Can Make You Happier," it reports a positive association between gratitude and happiness. According to the study, gratitude helps people feel positive emotions, cherish good experiences, improve health, handle adversity, and build strong relationships.[ix] We should be generous with gratitude. It does not cost a thing, but it is priceless. We need to show our sons how to live in a world of competing priorities with contentment and endurance in times of crisis. If parents understood suffering as a mechanism to build resilience and manifest higher potential in our sons, we would not hinder this rite of passage. Only a foolish person refuses to learn from their mistakes or the mistakes of others. Yes, there is a need for wisdom and discernment to avoid unnecessary suffering caused by choices we can control; however, not all periods of suffering can be controlled. The distinction between growth suffering and unnecessary suffering is the purpose of the pain and the maturity developed in it.

Parents are not always prepared to handle the struggles their sons may face. Sometimes it is a parent who unintentionally inflicts pain on their children. I made that mistake and it caused my son emotional pain. When Elijah was a toddler, he experienced severe separation anxiety during my military deployment. It was not diagnosed and we were not attuned to see the signs. I did my best to explain our upcoming separation but he did not seem to grasp it. Most toddlers cannot understand such things, so I thought he was 'too young' to be affected.

On the day of my departure, I went to hug my son, saying "See you later," and he appeared emotionless, with no facial expression. It was not the reaction I'd hoped for but I did not know how to respond to him either. So, I defaulted to what I was trained to do. I grabbed my duffel bags and walked out the door, leaving him standing with his dad. It was hurtful for me and I cried as I rode towards the airport. After ten minutes of tears, I shut down the mother in me and started thinking like the leader I was expected to be. I just switched gears, compartmentalizing that painful moment, preparing my mind to lead my team and head into a hazardous region. I could not focus on being Mommy; I was a military officer, responsible for the lives of others and supporting them throughout our deployment together.

Reunion with Elijah upon my return from deployment to the Middle East

Children are so imaginative and creative in the early years of life. In my private study time, I learned of the correlation beteween children's dreams and their mental health. They regularly operate in theta brainwave activity, which makes separating fact from fiction hard to do. Reflecting on my son's traumatic experience helped me understand that those long months of deployment to him were like 'losing his mom' and grieving. He could not discern the separation for work from the permanent loss of his mother. All he knew was that his mom went away for a long time and the separation left a significant mark on his life.

As parents, we may not know the lasting effects that show up at inopportune times in our children, frequently around the teenage years. As a college student, Elijah shared his past dreams, nightmares, and perceptions of that first separation experience. I was taken off-guard and deeply troubled, dare I say offended, by his 'memories.' I questioned his ability to separate reality from fiction, not understanding how those dreams were very real to him when he was four years old. All these years later, on the outside, he was a model son, but inwardly, he was in a battle. The pain he'd experienced was unintended. I had no way of knowing how my actions would affect his life, but as I listened to his story about those 'strange dreams' and nightmares, I realized they had.

Pride is like mold; it's ugly, it contaminates, and it grows until it is killed. There are times when we 'miss it' as mothers. In that season, I felt the weight of my son fighting a battle that should not have been his to fight and I was unable to fight it for him in his time of need. Sometimes, despite our best efforts as parents, we cannot stop the cause or continuation of our children's pain, and knowing my actions caused his pain was a heavy weight to bear. I had to ask for his forgiveness for the hurt I'd caused, even though I was trying to do something good for my country and my family. I did not apologize because I was wrong for serving in the military; I knew I was fulfilling my duty. I apologized because of the unintended consequences that resulted in his suffering. He needed my compassion, as his mother, to heal.

By humbling myself and acknowledging my role in his pain, it opened the pathway to forgiveness and recovery. Our path was not filled with roses; there were some challenging years that followed. It was not an overnight fix, and reconnecting with my son at times did not feel real. I had some angry, tormenting nights until I let go of what I could not control, the past, and forgave myself for what I deemed as my mistake.

Pride is like mold; it's ugly, it contaminates, and it grows until it is killed.

The Lord worked in me during this season of suffering to make Elijah not only more resilient, but also full of compassion and generosity. Although I can recall a number of times when I did not get mothering right, I am incredibly grateful and deeply humbled whenever I hear leaders tell me about Elijah's character and how well he represents our family. God works miracles, and my family is one of them.

In the 1990s, a song called "Joy and Pain" was popular. The lyricist contrasted the emotions of joy and pain to the experience of sunshine and rainy days. If parents desire to provide their children with a life devoid of pain and suffering, subconsciously, children may perceive life as a 'joyride' focused on their happiness without becoming equipped with the ability to process and grow through painful moments.

It is a responsibility to prepare our sons for suffering properly and using it purposefully. It is an instrument of their personal and professional leadership development. Over time and experience, different trials can lead to a far richer reward that is not duplicated in superficial luxuries. Many people who overcame personal adversities would not change their journey, despite their hardships, because they gained something invaluable in the process.

I do not enjoy seeing my sons suffer, but I would grieve the results of having sons who could not relate to suffering and the tough human experiences of others. My sons display empathy and consideration because they understand pain; I rejoice in that knowledge. I grew as a mother and a woman, suffering through this process with Elijah. We both discovered how to appreciate the opportunities before us. We are better individuals for going through our painful process together. We came through it wiser and more connected as mother and son. My gratitude for what remains good in our relationship and how suffering creates a deeper bond with my sons is a lifetime reward. I have faith we can endure future hardships because we endured them in the past.

For us, the best thing about Thanksgiving is giving thanks. It is not the fabulous food or football games. While those are blessings we enjoy, the real focus is the inward gratitude that compels us to be thankful for the people in our lives and the privileges we have. People with lives pointing towards gratitude combat the desires to overindulge or overextend themselves.

In this age of personal conveniences and immediate satisfaction, there is almost nowhere a person can go to get away from the access to everything at our fingertips. We have so much stuff of all kinds, all the time, good or bad, vying for our time, affection, and attention. Human appetites can be insatiable unless we restrain them, set boundaries, and take breaks to reorient our perspectives. Being content in life requires a lifestyle that practices being grateful for what we already possess and recognizing what makes living worthwhile. Our children are learning about values by watching their parents and others who influence their lives.

Let's not accept society's fluctuating message as the standard. Social media should not have a stronger influence over our children than the values we pass on to them. By proximity and exposure, children want the same level of material possessions and personal conveniences they observe, so the cycle of 'never content' repeats in the next generation unless we intervene. We live in a culture with less gratitude, more consumption, and a continual hunger and thirst that will not be filled by the things they possess.

Allow me to apply a motherly filter to Luke 22:31-32 that speaks to the spiritual fight for our sons:

> *Sisters, Sisters, Satan has asked to sift our sons like wheat but we are standing in prayer against his forces and interceding for them so their faith will not fail. As our sons turn to God, they will be strong and they will strengthen their brothers and sisters by leading well.*

Mothers fight for sons, the seed of Abraham. Our tenacity in prayer can break cultural, spiritual, and generational strongholds attacking our children. The price we pay as mothers for cultivating intimate relationships with God, and our sons, is insignificant compared to the benefits we gain.

Spiritual matriculation is vital to their overall health and development. People are spiritual beings who require nurturing, just as their minds need stimulation and their bodies require sustenance. It is easy to become fatigued in our human efforts as mothers, which never seem to be enough because they are not enough. We need reinforcements! Anyone who experiences warfare knows the value of having allies. Parenting is a battle, and who wants to fight a long war without allies? Every ceremony, tradition, or rite of passage we experience with our sons creates a community that supplies reinforcements to help us fortify them.

I desire for my sons to benefit from my struggles and bypass my mistakes; however, they have to take their own journey. When I got the revelation that my character could withstand certain situations due to the suffering I'd endured, it changed my perspective towards my sons. I allowed them more latitude to work through personal struggles, which teaches them how to recover from the consequences of making age-appropriate decisions. Is it easy? No, but it was necessary. My mothering instincts wanted to run to them and alleviate the hurt as fast as possible but I knew that in doing so, I would disrupt critical stages of their development and take away skills they needed for future success.

I also discovered some selfishness in the desire to want to alleviate my sons' pain. It provides a relief to me as a mother when I can quickly solve their problems. Then I can experience calm, redirect my energy, and focus on my own priorities. Mothering takes patience, and there is a reason patience is also called longsuffering. We cannot raise sons using microwave techniques and expect to produce men of standard. It takes time and repeated practice to cultivate a grateful attitude in our children. So, let patient mothering complete its work in developing grateful leaders who understand the privilege and responsibility in serving others. Let our sons go through the passage of some suffering, inconveniences, and struggles so they are capable of wielding weapons of sincere gratitude and resilience within their families and communities.

We cannot raise sons using microwave techniques and produce men of standard.

I learned obedience through training and discipline as a child. These principles showed me how much my family loved me, even when I resisted the process. Consider the amount of time and energy we invest into training our children; it is an act of love, even when it is painful for them. Children can be stubborn, and most children don't always obey the first time. Some of our sons insist on learning things from the 'school of hard knocks.' As one of my mentors would say jokingly, "This is a hard school to graduate from," but graduate they must. In the crucible of suffering, with gratitude, our sons can be transformed into men.

RITES OF PASSAGE

CHAPTER 9
PASSAGE OF GENERATIONAL COVENANT
ADOPTING DAUGHTERS-IN-LOVE

"If you want the cooperation of humans around you, you must make them feel they are important - and you do that by being genuine and humble."

Nelson Mandela

For this book, my primary focus was on mothering sons to become leaders and men of standard. I want to raise sons to be godly husbands who adore their wives and live in compassion towards their families. I want daughters-in-love (not law) to proudly bear our family name and experience true gratitude for being married to honorable men who lead well in their families with love, patience, and humility. I want to nurture sons who become courageous fathers, warriors who raise my grandchildren to be warriors too.

I foresee generational fruit being harvested from the seeds of integrity planted in our children. I am cultivating a bloodline covenant between two brothers who will remember, value, and pass down our family's

133

spiritual and natural legacies long after their parents are gone from this earth. I intend to raise godly, not perfect, children who seek to bring goodness to others. I want my sons, grandchildren, and their children to be visionaries from the beginning and manifest the promises of God in their lives, then show others the way.

After pondering on these grandiose thoughts, a question occurred to me: Who will my sons marry? They need women of equal mind, spirit, and purpose. My eldest son is in his twenties now, and is thinking about relationships and his future plans. He shared his heart with me concerning peer relationships, dating in particular. Because of his personal standards and the value he places on relationships, dating can be a minefield for him.

Our children are designed to be unique but being 'authentically you' is challenging in a superficial world.

My sons are not meant to be ordinary; neither are yours. Ordinary begets ordinary but to live abundantly requires living differently. Our children are designed to be unique but being 'authentically you' is challenging in a superficial world. Authentic living can create interesting dynamics and lonely times. I feel for my son, but I am encouraged in knowing his momentary suffering is producing in him a much greater desire to sacrificially love others including his future wife and children for the treasure they will be to him.

The joy he will have in the future will temper the memory of temporary loss and setbacks, but it is still hard to be patient waiting for a companion to walk in unity with him. It is a huge assignment to be a wife and mother, to live in unity with another person. Loyalty in relationships may result in scrutiny, bad advice, or criticism from people who are not on the same journey, especially in marriage. Sometimes, spouses must withstand well-intended attempts to 'protect them' that could undermine the unity in their marriage. As the main women in my sons' lives, their wives' belief in them plays a critical role in their success; it helps propel them to higher heights that may not be reached without their support.

I have little experience in raising a daughter, but I am a daughter, and I realize how important women are to creating the world we want to see. So daughters, you are not forgotten. In fact, I write because of you too. I want you to know good men exist. Never give up hope of marrying a man of standard who cherishes you for the jewel you are. Do not compromise your moral standards and hold men you are dating accountable for respecting you and demonstrating leadership that fosters productive relationships. You, my sisters, are worth it!

Rites of Passage

CHAPTER 10
PASSAGE OF FAMILY RITES
VISION CASTING

"Success leaves clues...it's not just about me."

Grandmaster Stephen Del Castillo

This sentiment was shared by the founder of my son's Blackbelt Leadership School during a Krav Maga Martial Arts promotion ceremony. Good parents are leaders who lovingly guide their families and unselfishly serve their communities. They advocate for others and operate with humility. Who doesn't love working with a gracious leader? People will run through brick walls for leaders who actually care about other people, their interests, and their ideas. Not enough of these leaders exist compared to the multitude of leaders who operate in vanity and self-serving philosophies.

Philippians 2:3-4 instructs all of us, including leaders: "Don't be selfish; don't try to impress others. Be humble, thinking of others as better than yourselves. Don't look out only for your own interests but take an interest in others too." Is this the attitude reflected in the leadership of your house, workplace, church, and community?

For most people it is not, because so many have stopped serving with humility and, by default, lead with pride, intimidation, and arrogance. Gracious leaders are high-value assets and we cannot afford to let them become extinct. This is one reason I hope to be an example of serving others through leadership instead of being a leader who treats others like my personal servants. It is the reason I want to have the dialogue about empowering principles in the rite of passage experiences.

On June 21, 2022, I celebrated 25 years of marriage, but the planning began three years earlier. I told Dave I wanted to do something to honor our commitment, our time, and the milestone of staying in covenant when we reached our 25th anniversary. We'd had our share of trials, but we also believed we would see our silver anniversary, and began casting a vision for what that moment could look like for us.

I definitely did not want another wedding ceremony. In fact, I was hesitant to have a ceremony at all. My preference was to elope, or more aptly, escape to a Caribbean island with a few friends and enjoy a week of fun and celebration. As a military couple, we'd had our wedding, then spent our initial days of marriage saying farewell to friends and family before relocating across the country. Not the honeymoon we pictured, but we made it work.

Dave had a different idea about how to celebrate our first 25 years. He wanted an anniversary event with friends and family but this time, our sons would be present. I was not keen on the idea until I considered what this moment could mean to our sons and their future roles as husbands and fathers. This event could be an opportunity for us to invite them to be a part of a family sacrament, and maybe they would be inspired to have their own 10, 15, 25, or 50-year vow renewal ceremony with their children someday. Since our sons would be of age to understand the significance of the occasion, they could play a critical part in making our anniversary celebration a family affair. This ingenious idea was catching on…and the Ferreira 'Rite of Passage' Silver Anniversary Gala was born.

We did not know what this event would ultimately evolve into, but we were determined to create something unique to our family covenant. We tossed around ideas for two years, until we were a year out and had to get serious with our planning. The traditional ceremony was a no-go: no white dress, tuxedos, or wedding marches. To define this moment, we began with our family vision and purpose. Why did this vow renewal ceremony matter at all, and what did we desire to accomplish? Once we aligned vision and purpose, the planning became easier and our path unfolded.

We decided our vow renewal would be presented in a multicultural family celebration with our community of friends. Coming off a few years of intense racial and cultural divides in America, we saw this as a personal invitation to create a unifying event, our part in bringing together people we love and respect from different backgrounds within our community and sphere of influence to commemorate the journey and the value of family. To set it apart, we included a diverse and inclusive message to welcome all our family and friends over the decades. Dave and I have different ethnic backgrounds. We have unique perspectives based on our upbringing, gender, culture, and individual personalities. Our anniversary gala acknowledged the beauty and shared values in these differences. We planned to focus on faith, culture, and community, with our sons there to experience the blessing of it all.

Our guests were invited to participate in the event by wearing their ethnic attire to the ceremony. They also gave tributes and we enjoyed the traditional line-dancing fun. After the ceremony was over, I was astounded by the impact it had on our guests and my family. Our sons truly leaned into the event, displaying their heartfelt joy for living in a family with committed parents who had weathered the storms. Sometimes, in the mundane of life activities, mothers may think the little things go unseen and do not matter to our children until we realize how much they really do notice.

The anniversary ceremony took me to a new height because we had no uncertainty about our vows, and we were walking in the fullness of our marriage commitment. We knew who we were and what we expected our family to become. Our renewed vows were spoken from a place of experience through joy, pain, and gratitude. They contained the beauty of sunshine and rain. Our sons had been participants in some of those complex rainy seasons. They could attest to our less-than-perfect family and need-some-work parenting skills, but they could also affirm our sincerity, faith, and love for one another.

Our family and friends were aware of some of our stories so they too rejoiced and celebrated with us, but no one knows you like the people who live in your house. Our renewal ceremony turned out to be as much of a family renewal as it was a reaffirmation of our marriage covenant. It was also a model to those present and living counterculturally in a world far too short on examples for marriage and family. That day was God's grace and mercy on full display.

We did not know that experiences like the rite of passage ceremonies would be so impactful and empowering. I want others to feel this experience and make it real for their marriages and families. I want you to imagine the generational blessings that come from parenting, covenant, and recognizing the milestones along the way. Most parents work to pass on traditions and hope their legacies outlive their lives, and this is the power in coming together to honor and celebrate milestones. I discovered that both rite of passage ceremonies, for our son and vow renewal, gave me more intimate connection and caused me to introspect more as a wife, mother, sister, friend, and leader.

Our rite of passage ceremonies did not have a formula; there was no secret ingredient. They were manifested out of timeless family moments. What made them timeless? We defined them and called them so, and our sons believed it. As mothers, we have creative ability in our words to speak dreams into our sons and call forth what we want to see in their future. It is why we choose their names with care, why we invest resources into training them, why we fight so hard for them. So, after all that is done, we cannot just walk away from our investment. We must make the impartation and pass the mantle in each ceremony. They become personal landmarks to remind them of their identity, purpose, and responsibilities. The ceremonies ensure the virtues and moments will not be easily forgotten or displaced.

How grateful I am to share these life-changing experiences. I want to leave you with a closing thought that mothers should ask ourselves routinely: What do you benefit if you gain the whole world but lose your son? A true power we possess as mothers is the influence we keep with our sons as they are developing into men. We are one example our sons need to see when it comes to serving, giving, and leading.

As mothers, we have creative ability in our words to speak dreams into our sons and call forth what we want to see in their future.

The rite of passage ceremony will not make your sons men, but it will set a demarcation line expressing love and support for their manhood. It can instill generational hope, traditions, and values, and I cannot think of a better way to love our sons than by celebrating their maturation into manhood.

In my journey as a mother, one lesson I know to be true is raising my sons to honor God first and love people always then, and only then, will they fulfill their calling to be men of standard.

Rites of Passage

What Others Are Saying About
Rite of Passage
Ceremonies
Vow Renewal

The Rite of Passage Anniversary Gala and Vow Renewal was inspiring in that it displayed how our traditions keep us together rather than tear us apart. Our cultures appear wildly different but actually, they ground us around core values of faith and family. I loved the incorporation of family into every aspect of the marital celebration. It showed how marriage is a continuation of the love of our ancestors and the future hope of our children. This celebration transcended time and space by gathering family and friends from across the country; it transcended generations by simultaneously showcasing their sons respect for their parents and the parents hope for their children; and it transcended cultures by honoring rituals from various people groups that inspired them along their way. This marital celebration was beautiful in every way possible.

Philip Page, Jr. –
Author, Getting Up Again

Family has always been the foundation of God's plan to fill the earth. The family system has been challenged in this time; however, despite the statistics and adversities marriages are still winning! I was a part of a beautiful 25th Anniversary Gala Vow Renewal ceremony with Dave, Sonya and their sons, Elijah and Ephraim. During the ceremony we sat there witnessing the beautiful colors that created such an awesome ambiance and music that set the atmosphere for a special evening and defining moment in their lives. Being in the presence of other guests, in their cultural attire, reminded us of our freedom and how we get to celebrate because of those who paid it forward. I loved the intimate moments and objects they incorporated to symbolize their love for each other and involving their sons in the ceremony was so heartfelt. My wife and I sat at our table just quietly discussing how this ceremony is definitely something we want as a tradition not only in our family but also in our marriage. They set the bar, not only how to love and serve each other but also how to celebrate the milestones and accomplishments in the journey. We are forever grateful to have witnessed such a beautiful ceremony. Thank you so much for your vision, your heart, and passion for community and celebrating life together.

May the Lord bless you and keep you, may the Lord make His face to shine upon you, and give you peace.

Dwane and Indera Cardenas –
Grace Family Church, Campus Pastor
and Beautiful Women's Group Leader

The 25th Anniversary Gala and Vow Renewal Ceremony was truly a demonstration of how culture and relationships founded in God aids in marriage longevity. As the day of the renewal ceremony was approaching, I did not know what to expect. I knew the typical itinerary would be a preacher and reciting of vows, like another wedding, for a couple re-establishing their love for each other. My assumption for this renewal ceremony was so wrong. Even though there was a preacher and vows were exchanged; there was a deeper sentiment about everything in the ceremony. Usually, vow renewal ceremonies focus on the special couple and very seldom have other people participate but not so with this event. Their plan deliberately included their family and community. The guests' interaction, even between strangers, led people to get more acquainted and connect with each other because of this family's vision for unity, community, and culture.

Lee Evans –
Author, Expanding the Kingdom

There are celebratory events that inform, inspire and educate while they entertain. This was one of those events. Marriage is questioned, inspected and criticized but not often enough celebrated. The Ferreira ceremony was able to shine a light on the joyous gift of marriage, the rewards of sharing your life with another and the accumulation of blessings over time. We are always a big proponent of marriage but this event was tangible evidence of its enduring value.

Robin Page –
Founder, College Hoodies for Kids (CH4K)

Rites of Passage

148

AFTERTHOUGHT
ACTION STEP/CHALLENGE

"Be Engaged: See something, Say something, Do something – make an impact around you."

Sonya D. Ferreira

I am often asked how to make the principles of this book practical to daily life. How can mothers guard our sons, and raise them to be men of standard and leaders with character? As a response, I included the following action steps to help mothers consider what they can start doing today to make an impact in the lives of our sons.

1. Be intentional about what we allow access through our son's senses, because some exposures are for their benefit, some are not, and both can have lasting implications.

2. Help them develop a mindset of choice so they are empowered to choose what to focus on and think about – society may teach other standards, tolerate cynicism, and engage in negativity by default, but mothers can encourage their sons to acknowledge facts while believing in the best outcomes and acting based on their values.

3. Consistently demonstrate behaviors and attitudes we want them to develop, like gratitude for the relationships and circumstances that grow their character – we have room to improve thankfulness in our personal and professional lives.

4. Teach them to recognize that pain and suffering are normal and happen as by-products of growth and living – pain and suffering can fuel purpose and passion, so use it to mature.

5. Evaluate how you can show up uniquely for your son(s) and what matters to them – monitor how you think and interact in your sphere of influence personally and professionally.

6. Show appreciation to people in your son's community who reinforce standards of excellence – thank them for being a source of encouragement, because everyone needs it.

CLOSING PRAYER FOR MOTHERS

Father,

Every person alive today is here because of a mother. I thank You for the gift of motherhood and for mothers who love, protect, and raise their sons to be men of standard. So often mothers carry the weight of raising children alone. They sacrifice and toil, hoping their childrens' lives will be better than their own.

I thank You for the wonderful example mothers set in parenting with sacrificial love like You showed us. Even when their situations are not ideal, help them press forward to overcome adversity. Use their disappointments and trying circumstances meant to break them and turn it into triumph and joy.

I ask You to continue to strengthen all mothers in their journey. Send them words of encouragement for the mundane as well as rewarding moments of mothering. When life is overwhelming or they feel tired and weary, refresh their minds and bodies to have renewed energy for the sake of their children.

Show mothers the right path to pursue and restore the peace in loving their families. Mothers are not perfect people and parenting is hard work. When they make mistakes, help mothers forgive themselves and extend grace so they can reconcile with their children and start again.

Restore broken relationships and release burdens for mothers who are disconnected from their families. Bring deliverance and comfort to mothers who are suffering, in bondage, or fighting through life's disappointments. Remind them of their value to You and the difference their presence makes in the lives of their children.

Help mothers partner with Your plan to produce godly sons who become men that honor their mothers in a way that pleases You. As mothers grow older, fill their sons and their wives with compassion to care for them. I thank You for hearing and answering when I pray.

In Jesus' Name,
Amen!

ENDNOTES

[i] Evans, Tony. (2019). The Tony Evans Study Bible. Used by permission of Holman Bible Publishers.

[ii] Johns Hopkins Medicine. (2023). Attention-Deficit/ Hyperactivity Disorder (ADHD) in Children. https://www. hopkinsmedicine.org.

[iii] Lewis, Robert. (1997) Raising a Modern-Day Knight. Used by permission of Focus on the Family, represented by Tyndale House Publishers.

[iv] Duffin, Erin. (Oct 12, 2022). Estimated Median Age of Americans at their First Wedding in the US from 1991 to 2021, by Sex.

[v] UK 2021 Census Data on Marriage Demographics Data and Analysis (2022).

[vi] US Census Data on Teacher Demographics (2021).

[vii] Disney, Thor. (2011). Marvel Studios.

[viii] Blackaby, H and Blackaby R. (1998). Experiencing God Day by Day. Used by permission of B&H Publishing.

[ix] Harvard Medical School. (August 14, 2021). Giving Thanks Can Make You Happier. Harvard Health Publishing. https://www.health.harvard.edu/health.

Suggested Reading

Eggerichs, Emerson. *Mother & Son: The Respect Effect.*

Eldredge, John. *Wild at Heart: Discovering the Secret of a Man's Soul.*

Farrar, Steve. *Anchor Man.*

Jakes, TD. *Disruptive Thinking.*

Lewis, Robert. *Raising a Modern-Day Knight: A Father's Role in Guiding His Son into Authentic Manhood.*

Maxwell, John. *Talent is Never Enough.*

Meyer, Joyce. *Battlefield of the Mind Devotional.*

Powell, Colin and Koltz, Tony. *It Worked For Me.*

Shirer, Priscilla. *Awaken.*

About the Author

Sonya D. Ferreira graduated with honors from Saint Mary's University in San Antonio, Texas with a Master of Arts degree in Counseling, specializing in Marriage and Family Therapy, and from Bowie State University with a Bachelor of Science degree in Psychology. With over 27 years of leadership and teaching experience, Sonya has cultivated a diverse perspective with unique insights into personal and professional relationships.

She is the visionary for Emissary Way which focuses on building bridges of connection and understanding through faith and practical principles for growing leaders in marriages, families, and communities. Her seminars are characterized by authenticity, humor, and transparency.

When she is not traveling, Sonya resides in Tampa, Florida with her husband, Dave, and their two sons, Elijah and Ephraim. She enjoys watching epic films, sports, and inspiring others through storytelling.

EMISSARY WAY

Building bridges of connection and understanding through faith and practical principles

EmissaryWay.com

 Emissary Way

 Emissary Way

 Emissary Way

 Emissary Way

 Emissary Way

www.ingramcontent.com/pod-product-compliance
Lightning Source LLC
Chambersburg PA
CBHW060523130626
46553CB00002B/631